Painting with a Needle

Painting
with a Needle

AN INTRODUCTION TO THE ART
AND CRAFT OF CREATIVE STITCHERY

NETTIE YANOFF BRUDNER

DOUBLEDAY & COMPANY, INC.

GARDEN CITY, NEW YORK

1972

I wish to acknowledge and express my deep appreciation
to my students in Gottschalk Junior High School, Louisville,
to teachers, museum officials, librarians
and friends for their ideas, help, encouragement,
and criticisms given during the compilation
of material used in this book. N.Y.B.

ISBN: 0-385-09206-7

Library of Congress Catalog Card Number 79–180117

This book is dedicated to those who seek
to interpret and share their discoveries
of the designs of the world around us.
This book is for you, the beginner in stitchery.

CONTENTS

PART THREE DISPLAYING A STITCHERY

APPENDIX

ILLUSTRATIONS

PART ONE

Discovery Through Stitchery

INTRODUCING YOU TO STITCHERY

Stitchery is not a new art but one which we can trace back at least to the times described in the Old Testament. The Book of Exodus tells us "And he made a veil of blue, and purple, and scarlet, and fine twined linen: with cherubims made he it of cunning work" (36:35) and "the hanging for the gate of the court was needlework, of blue, and purple, and scarlet, and twined fine linen." (38:18.) Tabernacle hangings, couch covers, clothes and tents were found in the royal tombs of Ur. The background fabric was linen, decorated with appliqué, gold plate, wire and goat's hair, and the colors used were scarlet, blue and purple—identical to those mentioned in the Bible. Bronze needles that date back to before Christ were excavated at Mohenjo-Daro in India. These needles were used in decorating textiles and measured three millimeters. Needles have been made of fish bone, splinters of wood, and other natural materials and have been found in the ruins of Pompeii, along with thimbles, tweezers and bodkins.

The oldest stitch on record is thought to be the Chain Stitch, used, some say, first by the Chinese. The Egyptians, too, used it in giving the sails of their ships better support and "give" with the wind. Dating back to the second to fourth century A.D., tunics, wall hangings, covers, cushions and church vestments embroidered and appliquéd using the Chain Stitch on heavy twill, silk, linen, wool and felt were found in the Crimea. Fragments of embroidered silk were found in a grave at Kerch, and they showed figures and ornaments done in East Indian designs with the Chain Stitch.

Each civilization developed special techniques, designs, fabrics and combinations of materials which were suitable in expressing their ideas. Conditions that existed during each period had much to do with the type of work that was created. Therefore, the stitcheries of some eras have been more elaborate than others, but each has left works of art characteristic of the age. As William Morris wrote in *Needlework in Religion*, "To know that men lived and worked mighty before you is an incentive for you to work faithfully now, that you may leave something to those who come after you."

Having seen fourth-century robes of the types described in Exodus and the famous Bayeux Tapestry enhanced with embroidery, I was inspired, but these pieces were not examples of the kind of stitchery I thought suitable for me to attempt. It somehow brought back memories of childhood, when Mother would buy articles with designs stamped on them to keep her children usefully occupied. For reasons which I only now understand, I objected to these set patterns. I loved even then to add embroidery to a belt, headbands, collar or pocket, using my *own* design with a Back or Outline Stitch, easy and natural to do, for one of my duties was to help put hems in clothing made for us. No, stitchery is not a new art for me, either. In high school I had the opportunity to make a simple design on fabric; transferring a crayon design and using my favorite Outline Stitch with the embellishment of the Chain and French Knot stitches, I produced a small pocketbook. I discovered what a beautifully designed tool is the needle and all it can be guided to do. Think of all the magic people have worked with it. And later I was fortunate to have had a friend who had taken lessons from a European peasant and was willing to share her knowledge. A few basic stitches, variations and combinations of each—this was the beginning of experimenting with stitchery, which has been developing from pastime to an important part of my life.

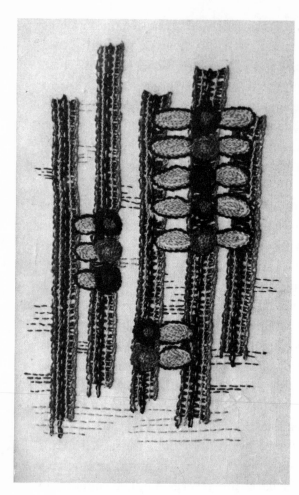

An abstract pattern—
synchronization—
originated with a
sketch of traffic
lights.

You too will be amazed at the many designs you can produce, and this book is planned to give you the necessary stimulation. This invitation to creating with fabric, needle, thread and yarn is the beginning. The inspiration behind this form is artistic, personal and carefree embroidery. We'll consider the basic techniques to achieve our desire, the communication of what we see and feel, and to start you off, perhaps, you will be able to follow step by step a number of designs. Each stitchery has a list of supplies, patterns and instructions to show how a stitchery develops from idea to finishing touches of steam pressing and framing or hanging.

One does not need to master all the stitches of crewel embroidery in order to be creative and produce a stitchery of high quality. I do teach my students to set their goals high and do all they can to reach them, but not to become discouraged if they don't; they will learn a lot along the way, and that is an important fact in creative stitchery. Some people are inhibited by fear of making mistakes, but a person who makes no mistakes does nothing. Some of the most unusual stitcheries are created accidentally: Make use of opportunities and examine errors made to see if they can lead into invention.

"I could never do that—I always need patterns for everything I do, someone else's patterns. Nettie proceeded to prove me wrong. She demonstrated and opened our minds and eyes as to how original patterns for needlework could be accomplished. Looking at specimens from nature, keeping in mind the basic shapes, using few kinds of stitches, allowing the design to evolve. Much to my amazement I started with the form of a starfish which ended up being a clown! An eggplant on the kitchen table was translated to cloth with a few simple stitches. The scene viewed from my front door was put down by my ten fingers on cloth, using the Chain Stitch. Here I was, heretofore locked into a set pattern, and now I am absolutely free to express my own ideas and imagination, to create my own designs."

These kind and enthusiastic words from a lady in a group meeting at my home reflect the joy of self-expression. Most crewel designs have a great deal of detail work and pre-planned colors and shading, keeping you restricted to materials and patterns in kit or traditional design. When you work on a fixed design, you do miss the intimacy with subject matter, no matter what other satisfactions that kind of

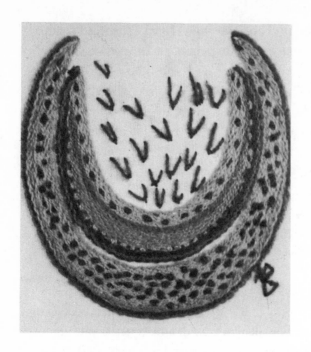

This basic letter "C" becomes a slice of melon.

embroidery provides. Free to do your own thing, you feel closer to nature, forms and emotions than ever before. Creating leads to learning. Becoming selective in what we wish to capture is learning to make decisions. The characteristic quality of my own work, for example, comes from discovery of the fundamental shapes of all things. When we learn to use our senses fully and observe natural and man-made objects closely and freshly, we see repetitions of shapes, lines and colors, we sense rhythms and related forms in quite different areas of life. One can make a whole series of fruit designs easily by beginning with the shapes of letters of the alphabet or geometric forms. A stitchery, "Gladiator," was first inspired by consideration of the shape and intricacy of a particular TV aerial. The sources of inspiration, not least of course museums and printed works, really are boundless, just waiting for the eye and needle of the adventurous—you.

DISCOVERING DESIGNS

Design is everywhere, but most of us never take the time to make this discovery. How many times had I picked dandelions from the lawn without realizing what beautiful plants they were. Then, I discovered that a weed is as exquisite in design as a cultured flower. It all happened one summer day. While relaxing in the sun, I saw that right before my eyes, between the woven strips of a lounge chair, was a circle of green leaves and in the center were brilliant yellow flowers: dandelions. I decided to examine this plant more closely. The whole was so artistically arranged. It was like a corsage with a few blossoms set in the center of triangular-shaped leaves graduating in size. Examining one plucked flower still more closely, I saw its composition, many small oval petals grouped together to form a spiked round. My impression of dandelions—and the extraordinary common beauty they sym-bolize—changed that day. Dandelions are not weeds but lovely plants that spread their sunshine over the soft brown soil of our earth.

Design is everywhere. You must have stopped, on a clear summer night, to look up at twinkling stars and wonder. I have, and my way of expressing thoughts and feelings about stars is making various designs to symbolize them. Snowflake, tumbleweed, star-type flower designs use different com-binations of color, Chain, Outline and French Knot stitches, but each was started from the center of the design.

According to the chronological plan of creation, the flora —grasses, trees, flowers and fruits—were created first. Next came fauna—sea, land and air creatures—which enhanced the earth's environment. Man was then created to observe, utilize and enjoy. Treat yourself to close observation. Take a vegetable or fruit; look at the basic shape as a whole,

then cut it in half. Cut one piece lengthwise and you will discover completely different designs. Some evergreen pods, when cut lengthwise, reveal an intricacy within which reminds one of a stringed musical instrument. The strawberry is heart shaped and the tiny green shoots are so evenly spaced. The leaves arranged around the stem are so perfectly balanced in size and color. Small wonder this fruit is such a favorite stitchery subject.

Start studying everything around you as if you were a detective looking for clues. Indeed, sometimes a magnifying glass does help uncover some of the mysteries. Try using an inexpensive microscope; the unusual patterns now seen can be effectively translated. Even with the naked eye, take note of contrasts in colors and the lines, ridges and textures of each specimen. Did you realize a person can see his world as a camera does? You will want to look at the same object in different ways; try squinting, for you often want not the details as the jumping-off point but the basic shape.

An airplane trip will provide dozens of stitchery designs. The patchwork of cultivated fields, curve of mountain ranges, stream of traffic, rows of houses or industrial buildings, circles and squares of new suburban developments—the linear pattern and bas relief of the earth below are fascinating studies.

The seasons of the year can be a guide in helping you select shapes, colors and textures for a stitchery. In winter, the lines of bare deciduous trees are especially striking; frost and icicle patterns also come quickly to mind. The colors of winter are subtler, perhaps, but stitcheries using monochromatic schemes and various textures are very beautiful. And before you know it, the bud and bloom of spring are at hand. And then summer, with the year's fullest range of colors, is nudged by autumn, favorite season of so many. Harvest is but one design related to the fall and pictured in this book. Inspiration abounds, even in an ear of corn, each kernel a carved design of great beauty. Examine closely a stalk, with its shucks and silky hair.

Trees and some plants, such as the ivy vine, with its repeated shapes, fantastic range of color from light green to red, span the seasons as sources of stitchery designs.

Pictured here is one of the most realistic trees I have done: Autumn Aglow, in browns and oranges. Good subjects are bamboo, for its simple, long oval leaves and thick stems with deep ridges; weeping willow, for its grace; palm, magnolia, evergreens, birch and all fruit trees. Pine, oak and the oak's acorns are of course popular themes; consider, as well, the unusual ginkgo, the beech, or perhaps the tree's nuts, needles, roots or berries.

Possibilities among the flowers can only be touched upon: easy shapes of tulips, iris, penny flower (symbol of honesty), Queen Anne's lace, exquisitely delicate babies'-breath, sunflowers, cattails, bleeding hearts, water lilies. . . .

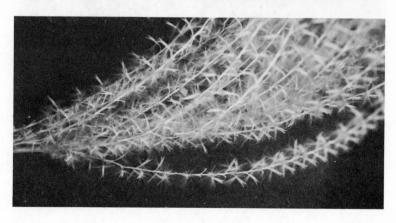

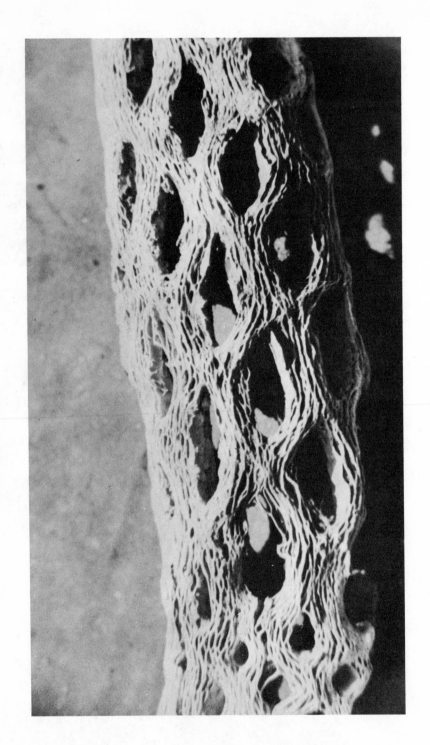

DISCOVERY THROUGH STITCHERY

There are grains, vines and the interesting patterns of vines twined about stems, and vegetables, from the common potato, here shown in graceful sprouting, to the mushroom, and four-leaf clover symbols of good luck, to squash, onions, peppers, etc. Take time to see the contrast of tones on the mushroom, its domelike top; enjoy the contrast of thicknesses and linear patterns when an onion is sliced or the lines observed when an onion's skin is held up to the light. Gradually one becomes clever in seeking out natural resources of various regions such as the repeated pattern in the latticelike form, opposite, or in "helping nature along," by arranging pressed flowers and foliage, or using man-made symbolic designs such as a door decoration in the shape of a Christmas tree and constructed with real leaves.

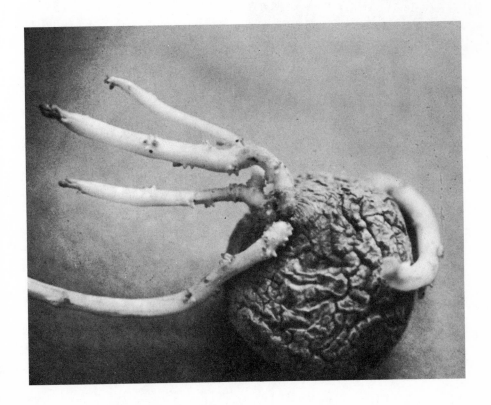

Although one type or another seems popular at any given time or has evolved as symbolic such as the owl, each species within the animal kingdom lends itself beautifully to creative stitchery. Domestic, farm or zoo, tame or wild: rabbits, squirrels, turtles and snails; dove, turkey, swan, cardinal or pheasant; seahorse, starfish, lobster or octopus.

You can be as faithful or imaginative as you wish, using subject as departure point. I happen to love the parrot, for its exquisite contrasts in color and unusual bill make an interesting subject. The owl's large eyes can be exaggerated in so many different ways. Peacock designs can be as breathtaking as nature's own. The framed stitchery opposite shows one possible interpretation of a feathered creature.

Big Blue Owl

One reward of close observation—or creative viewing—would be appreciation of the forms and designs insects provide. The bee's hexagon-shaped honeycomb may come immediately to mind. Such patterns as this or the inner spiral of a shell have long been used by architects and are all about us. All of the following insects are fascinating not only in shape but in color and pattern: spiders and their webs, cicadas with their transparent wings, grasshoppers, fireflies, butterflies and ladybugs.

We have considered the uses of vision and the parallel of eye and camera. Nature viewed close up or from afar will provide endless inspiration. The original motivation or inspiration of the stitchery Harvest, shown in color in this book, was awareness of land formations, curves, hills and valleys seen in Montana and other places. Similarly, the waves, bubbles, foam and splash of water as a ship or boat leaves port create patterns. Illustrated is an extremely simple collage in shades of blue which uses or interprets this pattern. Tracks left by cars in snow or dried mud or by animals have given me several stitchery ideas.

It's impossible to list the ideas nature provides, but here is a sampling:

> Twinkling stars in a deep blue sky on a clear night, or cloud formations whose interesting shapes keep changing with the wind. Again, your mind can wander from observation to fantasy; the stitchery here is almost free form but stems from memory of celestial pattern.
>
> Striking shadows formed by sun, moon or artificial light.
>
> Ploughed fields forming curved and even rows.
>
> Land formations: mountains, peaks and table-flat areas, high and low areas.
>
> Circular ripples from a dropped pebble, oil on the water's surface.

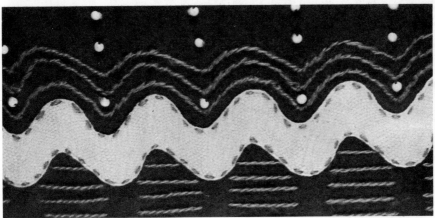

Dried mud puddles with their wavy and curved lines.
Bales of hay or stacks of corn so evenly and neatly ar-
ranged.
Oceans at different times of day or in storm.
Birds sitting on fence or telephone wire.

Stitcheries can record impressions, vacations, feelings. They
can as well interpret objects viewed on trips to the museum, botanical garden or aquarium. They can grow from
photographs in science books, old lithographs or newspapers.

The Gladiator

They can range over the infinite variety of the world, or give added dimension to some special interest or hobby of your very own.

Perhaps the greatest opportunity for creativity lies in observing and interpreting man-made objects. In "Ways to Begin a Design," we will explore techniques of translating observations. You can paint a still life with a needle, make the actual abstract, by using repetitions of patterns as in Traffic Lights, or building upon basic shapes, such as letters of the alphabet. As previously explained, The Gladiator began with the curved shape of a TV aerial.

Viewing the Lazy "K"
Teapot on its side reveals
the source of the pattern
within the pot.

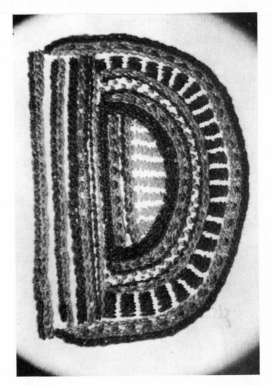

A SYMBOL FOR YOUR THOUGHTS

From the beginning of time, when man wanted to express his thoughts, ventures in life or discoveries, he found a way to share his ideas with others through the means of symbols. Symbols are simply pictures that tell a story briefly; they can be in outline form so that just the shape will suggest something. An example would be a circle with lines radiating from it, to represent the sun. Such drawings can be understood by anyone regardless of age and the language he speaks.

The lotus flower of Egypt was the symbol of the sun, because it opened in the morning and closed in the evening. At a later date the lotus became the symbol of the continuing cycle of life. Through the ages, flowers, objects, even colors have come to make statements beyond their representational value. Myrtle, for instance, stands for love and victory. Its constancy and immortality are common to other evergreens.

Here is a brief list of symbols adaptable to many occasions and individuals you might wish to honor with a stitchery:

Apple: Life, mankind.

Chain: Strength.

Circle: Sun, cycle of life, wheel of fortune, eternity, union.

Clasped hands: Friendship, brotherhood.

Dove: Peace, love, affection.

Ivy: Long life.

Lamp: Guiding light, knowledge.

Lily: Madonna.

Lion: Strength, courage.

Marigold (or sunflower): Affection, gratitude.

Oak leaf: Honor, strength, glory.

Olive tree: Peace, plenty, victory, wealth, tree of life, wisdom.

Owl: Wisdom.
Palm: Peace, victory.
Pansy: Thoughtfulness.
Peacock: Immortality.
Penny flower: Honesty.
Pine cone and pomegranate: Fertility, regeneration.
Red roses: Love, beauty, affection.
Scarab beetle: Good luck.
Torch: Eternal life.
Wheat: Productivity, life, autumn.
Willow (or cypress): Sadness, mourning.

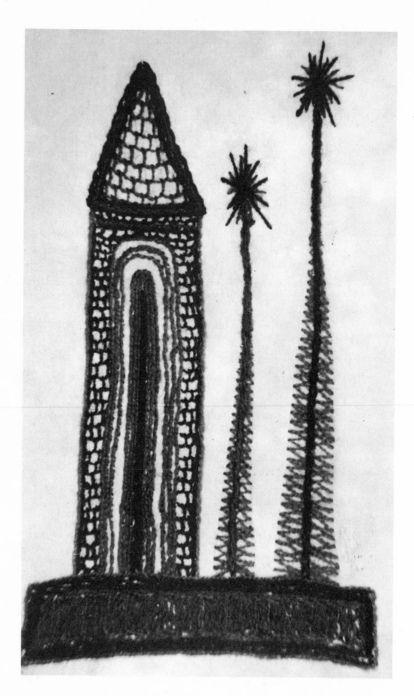

This imaginative representation of a typical storybook castle is useful as a symbol for "home." I actually used the entrance to my Tudor-style home for inspiration.

Reading about folk art of each region of the world will provide still other examples of symbols and appreciation of the fascinating universal meanings of so many types.

Merely the color used connotes much such as blue for coolness, truth or honesty; red for fire, love, life; white for purity, peace and holiness; yellow for warmth; gold for honor, respect, goodness. Purple often signifies royalty; rose, beauty; green, life, birth and growth. The psychology of color is a study in itself and beyond this book.

The possibilities are so numerous that it is wise, when first getting into stitchery, to limit yourself to a few favorite colors. If you tend toward autumn and earth tones such as tans, rusts, browns, golds, oranges and greens, you still have a wide range. You can avoid bewilderment at first by choosing colors that belong to one family. In selecting colors, remember that black and white are not considered colors and so you can work them into a design and still have a one-color stitchery.

Try making your own discoveries of the power of color. Sir Isaac Newton found the complete range when he held a piece of glass up to light and saw a colorless fragment turn into a rainbow of shades. No better place exists for ideas for color combinations than nature itself. The beautiful blend of golds and purples of a pansy; the blues, lavenders, pinks and deep purples in the morning glory; the range contained in just one autumn leaf . . . all these combinations are effective, regardless of the subject. How lovely and cool are the off-white water lilies with bits of green and blue, how soft the gradation of silky gray pearls on the pussy willow. What better contrasts than those of monarch butterflies, parrots and peacocks.

Colors are like actors on stage, each one contributing his part and no one finishing until each has had his turn to appear.

WAYS TO BEGIN A DESIGN

The Olive Tree, on the opposite page, represents the use of symbolism (in this case, plenty, victory, the tree of life), favorite autumn colors, and one easy way of setting down a design—arrangement of cutout shapes on fabric. Other methods are direct sketching on the background fabric, transferring a design and doodling or developing free forms.

The Olive Tree also represents my first stitchery and was preceded by a great deal of research into descriptions of various types of the tree, and its importance in biblical history. The background fabric is pure Belgium linen purchased in a decorator's shop, and the embroidery was done with crewel yarns in browns, rusts and oranges. Many patterns of olive leaves were cut and pinned to the material and after arranging them satisfactorily, I used the Running Stitch to outline the leaves, olives and branches. The trunk and branches were worked with the Chain Stitch, always starting at the base and working up, the way things grow, up toward the sun for warmth and strength. The olives were done in two shades of orange, using the French Knot. And the finished whole incorporates all I had learned of the olive tree, with its long, oval pointed leaves and close-grained wood—but it clearly was my interpretation. This is what creative stitchery is all about.

Through your observations of natural and man-made articles and arrangements, you will note harmony, color and functional or frivolous designs. In using these observations to create with a needle, you need only please yourself; you are experimenting each time you begin a design and in this regard free arrangements with bits of paper or fabric are as stimulating as sketches in your notebook of observations. Each has its place and value.

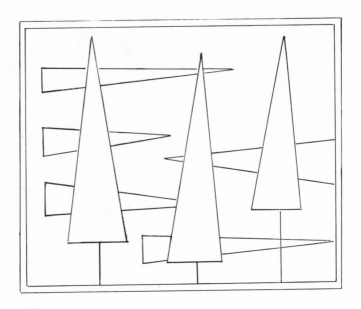

PAPER PATTERNS OF BASIC SHAPES

No more direct use of awareness of basic shapes in our environment is possible than through this method. As in the case of The Olive Tree, making paper patterns can *aid* the composition of your design. Begin exploring by cutting some paper patterns, making at least three different sizes of each shape. Brown wrapping pattern has the needed sturdiness; colored construction paper is good and guides color selection and placement. Try grouping shapes and overlapping others. The pattern can then be "transferred" to the fabric by light pencil marks, or by Running Stitches which can either be eventually removed or made part of the design.

An Evergreen design, done with the Herringbone Stitch and framed by the Outline Stitch, is one simple example of an arrangement of like shapes. You will be better off keeping your composition rather simple. Illustration above.

A drawing or painting you have done can also be used for a stitchery by this method. It (or a tracing of it) can be cut up and used as a pattern. It could become more abstract if you use a darker color yarn between the cutouts, to represent a leaded stained-glass window. It is interesting to note that Rouault worked as a designer of such windows and his paintings reflect that, in turn.

The Castle, below, was based on an arrangement of paper patterns. Various sizes of gray and black rectangles were glued onto paper and this served as a guide in making the original outline. The pattern was pinned in place and torn away once the Running Stitch marked the outline. After working the different areas with several colors and stitches,

I felt the design resembled a building. As it happened, the architectural decoration of a particular motel suggested a castle and this was the inspiration for the finishing touches on this place. Almost any outline or basic shape is ideal for filling in—as we saw with alphabets and teapots.

The cut paper shapes naturally do not have to be the standard geometric forms. If you fold a piece of paper one time or several times, you will have a design that is symmetrical or repeated. The black and white pattern shown is one example and may remind you of an ink blot. This is the same principle as the one used in making paper doilies. This is what you will want for butterflies, masks, insects, etc. It is very effective when used in a stitchery incorporating a name or monogram. The letter "B" lent itself nicely to the folded paper pattern method; the stitchery shown is done in various tones of peach and brown on beige linen.

With this, as with other methods, planning your design is like planting a seed and watching it grow: Use instincts and whims and add or subtract to your pattern as you like.

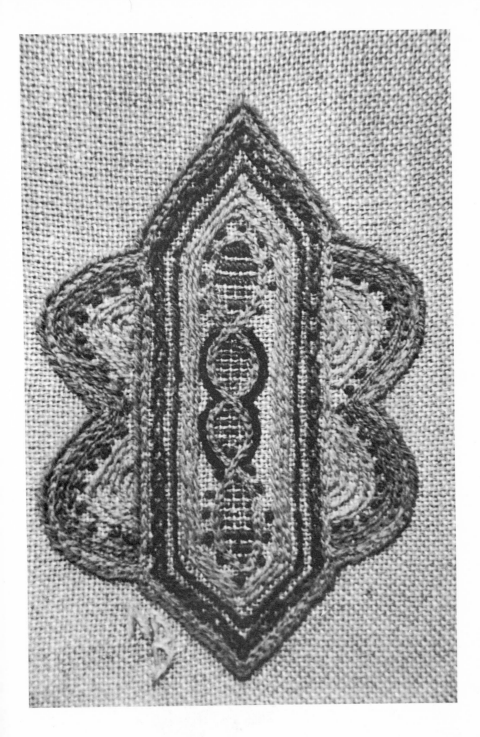

Surely you have idly let your pencil wander during a telephone chat, lecture or meeting. One of the most common forms doodling takes is elaboration of a letter. The stitchery monogram "C" uses the Chain Stitch alone; somehow this helps underscore its source as penciled embellishment on the basic shape of the letter.

Creating a line design is something like doodling. You start with a line. It can be straight, curved, thick, thin, long, short. Lines can be broken into parts, evenly or not. They can be repeated. And they can be grouped. Spaces between them can vary to define the pattern of lines so that you see at once they symbolize waves or rays, etc.

Patterns of lines create background but even as such can be carefully made part of the central design. Repeated squares of short straight lines, alternating in direction (horizontal and vertical), looked like woven fabric and were the appropriate background for a stitchery of a spider, entitled The Weaver.

Lines can be used in combination with geometric shapes or used to fill in those shapes. They can graduate in size to form shapes of their own.

Lines can go in opposite directions, or they can combine to lead to a focal point.

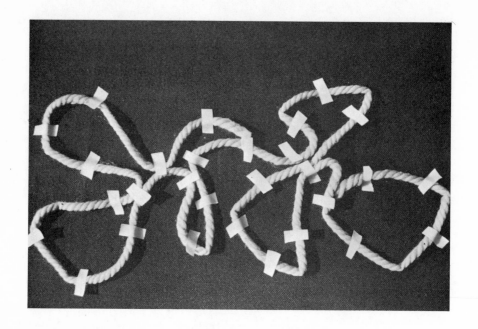

You can sometimes start with a doodle design and then look for interesting shapes within it. These can be set off by shading with pencil or crayon. Shapes can be repeated by simply using tracing paper and transferring them where you wish. Two or three forms can also be combined into a single larger form. It is wisest to plan a design of this type on paper first.

When you become more experienced, line and free-form designs can be drawn directly on background fabric, using chalk or pencil—or the yarn itself. Make swirls and loops with yarn, adjusting the design until you are satisfied with it. You do have control of your yarn making this type drawing. The thick yarn used in the Free Form design, in Part Two and in the color section of this book, was taped in place, as you see. It can also be pinned before being stitched down. Such designs are striking when careful selection of shades of one or two colors is made.

An artist keeps a sketchbook of ideas which he refers to at times, but scratch pads measuring 4 by 6 inches are handy to carry. With pen or pencil, one can make a quick sketch of things that appeal, adding notes if you wish. Once home, you can place each sketch in alphabetical order, behind cards with titles of larger categories such as "Nature Designs, "Man-made Designs," etc.

Start collecting specimens of nature, collections of shells, rocks, fossils, pine cones, driftwood and ever so many other things—pressed flowers, butterflies, dried specimens and so on.

Start collecting pictures that interest you in magazines and newspapers, keeping them labeled in a box or file.

Visit museums and all places giving you the opportunity to view sculpture, paintings, artifacts and of course all types of stitchery and accessories. Start delving into primitive art books; the simplicity in this type of painting, crafts and needlework is educational and inspiring.

And practice using a camera. Any one will do for your reference file; naturally, close-up lenses will record detail of texture as found on rock formations you really cannot bring home!

In this first part are a few photos I have made for stitcheries —some day.

Make some sketches looking at the subject from different angles. If the subject happens to be a fruit, flower or vegetable, make a sketch of the whole and a cross section. Examine inside as well as outside. Use the natural growth system from seed or bulb to full-grown plants. Seeds, stems, roots and leaves can be included in the design. A pineapple has so many geometric shapes, textures and colors that it would be an excellent specimen from nature to start to use in de-

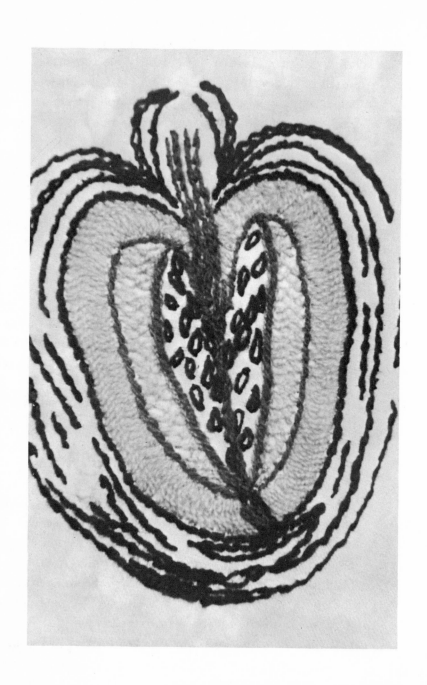

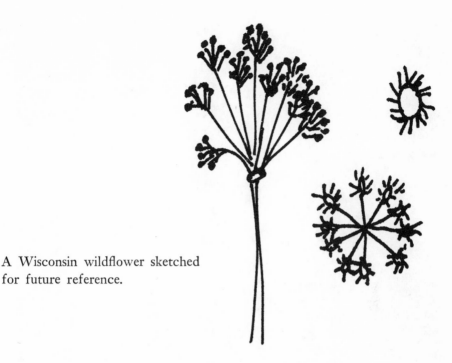

A Wisconsin wildflower sketched
for future reference.

signing. The shape of the fruit as a whole represents an oval.
Each diamond in the covering has wonderful possibilities
and colors ranging from dark gray to light green and brown,
depending on ripeness. Even if you do not follow the shape
of this particular fruit, it offers a palette of colors to work
with.

You can't beat nature for organization and right proportion. The closer you observe these things, the sooner you will
discover that you too can begin a design with ease and
confidence. Step back and take in the branch system or root
growth of a tree. Bend over and examine the arrangement
of petals on a flower.

Learn to look through the eyes of a child. Put down only
essential lines and shapes. That is one reason I sometimes suggest using a crayon in place of pen or pencil. The thicker

DISCOVERY THROUGH STITCHERY

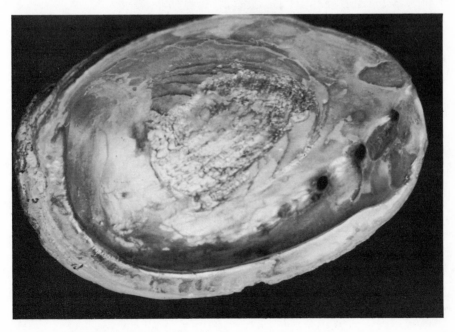

Designs are sometimes suggested when you help nature along, as in the collage opposite.
Objects around the home are another fine source of inspiration. Pictured here are an antique comb and a tile from a mantelpiece.

lines and usually more primary color get you away from trying to mimic Michelangelo, or nature. Let your honesty and imagination come through. As a beginner, sketch some simple objects and make as many as you feel you need before you can visualize what you are aiming to record. Then try to draw the objects from memory, using basic shapes only. Remember, geometric forms, not realistic ones. To achieve a center of interest, look for one shape or group of shapes that does attract the eye.

You may need time to study your subject before beginning a design, for you may have to figure out a way to simplify it. I can only repeat what I have found to be true: The general basic shape is the answer, the departure point. As you stitch, the freedom of this craft will let the design evolve naturally. That's the fun of it, keeping yourself open for new ideas.

Remember, nature has rhythm, repeated shapes or natural growth movement such as winds making ripples in a meadow. After you have set down the basic design on your fabric, using a simple Running Stitch, your needle can then really become the artist's tool. Do remember, then, to give yourself enough background room so your design can grow; I failed to do this at first and was not able to explore further but was forced to make an abrupt stop.

A good composition must have unity, orderly arrangement and balance, but with nature as your guide, you will not go far wrong. You may, for example, have a beautiful shell, which would be excellent as a subject with its repeated lines. The same idea can be carried over into the filling in of background, if you wish, but you would exaggerate the lines. Or take a piece of wood, with its grains forming the design. That, too, can be interpreted with thread and needle, but it is only the beginning of an idea which can be developed.

Some artists like to make a full-scale sketch of their design before even attempting to start with the main project. Tapestry weavers make an outline of the shapes of areas to be woven, and this guide is called a cartoon. To do this or not is your decision. This book offers no set rules, but suggestions and records of one woman's experiences and discoveries. You will want to make your own.

TRANSFERRING A DESIGN

SUPPLIES NEEDED

> Clean flat hard surface
> Transparent parchment tracing paper or substitute
> Clear matte spray fixative or substitute (hair spray)
> Masking tape
> Wrinkle-free background fabric
> Dressmaker's carbon paper: yellow or white for dark fabrics
>   and red or blue for white or light-color fabrics
> Colored ink ball-point pen

STEPS IN TRANSFERRING A DESIGN

Transferring a design onto background fabric is simple to do if you follow these instructions:

Place a piece of tracing paper over the complete design. Use a pencil to trace over every line of the design. If you find the tracing paper slipping, just use a few paper clips to hold it in place. This usually presents no problem, as tracing paper is so transparent, and you should have no trouble getting it back in place.

You will find it most worth-while if you spray the tracing paper (with complete design on it) with clear matte spray fixative or substitute. Follow directions on can of fixative if you plan on using it. The reason: This keeps the penciled design from rubbing off or smudging. It is much quicker than having to go over design with pen and ink.

Next place the wrinkle-free fabric (press if necessary) top side down (if there is a difference) on a clean hard surface such as a table, heavy cardboard or possibly your kitchen

floor. Use some strips of masking tape across the corners of the fabric to hold it in place and to keep it from slipping around while transferring the design.

Put the carbon paper on top of the taped-down fabric, remembering, of course, to have the carbon side facing down toward the fabric. It is *important* that the carbon paper stay in place while tracing the design. To ensure this, place strips of masking tape across the corners of the carbon paper.

Place the piece of tracing paper with the design on top of the carbon paper, which has been taped down on top of the fabric. Once the design on the tracing paper is centered, tape its corners down with masking tape. This keeps everything together in one place.

In the final step, you will be transferring the design onto the background fabric. It is suggested that you use a red ink, ball-point pen so that if you are interrupted, you will know where you were when you return. To trace over the design, be sure to make slow, smooth, but firm strokes with the pen. *Note:* Be sure that you do not miss going over a single bit of the design, as these strokes are putting onto the fabric (via the carbon) the exact design you will soon be stitching. In fact, as a precaution, you should trace over the design twice to make sure that all of it goes onto the fabric.

Remove the masking tape from the corners of the tracing paper, carbon paper and the fabric with the design on it.

To keep the fabric from raveling while you are stitching, place some masking or magic transparent tape along the cut edges. These strips come off easily after you have finished your stitchery.

INCREASING OR DECREASING SIZE OF A DESIGN

You may have a design which you would like to decrease or increase in size and use it as a stitchery pattern. This can be done very easily, if you follow these simple instructions.

If design cannot be folded, draw some lines up and down (vertically) and also across (horizontally), using a pencil and ruler to measure equal number of spaces between each block.

On another piece of paper, mark off the same number of spaces that was made on the original design. Only the size blocks will be different.

Label each block. Numbers can be used across the top side and letters can be used on the side from top to bottom.

Note: Graph paper can be used. Transparent tracing paper can be placed over original design, if you do not want to mark on it.

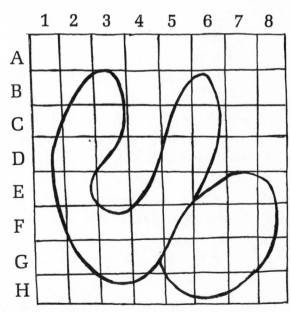

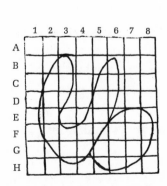

CREATIVE USES FOR STITCHERIES

Creative stitchery is painting with a needle and it thus follows that you often wish to frame your finished piece. Part Three of this book tells you all you need to know to finish an appropriate frame. But in addition, many useful and attractive articles can be made for yourself and others to enjoy. The time spent in making your own design is well worth it and the satisfaction is guaranteed.

Below is a list of ideas for articles and apparel that can be made more beautiful with stitchery. And more fashionable—look how appliqué and embroidery have re-emerged to give all-important unique touches to clothes in the seventies.

Aprons	Banners	Beach bags
Bedspreads	Bellpulls	Belts
Blouses and sweaters	Bookmarks	Headbands
Curler bags	Guitar straps	Place mats
Jewelry boxes	Picture frames	Screen panels
Pillows	Pin cushions	Hangings
Purses	Pot holders	Curtains
Skirts and pants	Handkerchiefs	Religious articles
Towels	Dresses	Trinket boxes

Obviously you can enhance bought articles, or you can make something from scratch. A bellpull is an easy project; a length of material thirty-six inches is fine. For a belt, measure the waist, decide on the width and add two inches to each dimension for seams (cut a lining of unbleached cotton one inch smaller than the belt). Turn under one inch on all sides, using mercerized thread to match color of the belt, pin lining in place and sew on by hand with an embroidery crewel needle. It can be held together with hook and eyes or yarn ties to match the stitchery.

Border designs are perfect for belts, bellpulls and many

other things. The design can be planned to fit between narrow or wide, straight or curved lines. It can be anything which bears repeating, including symbols. Perhaps it is easiest to plan it first on paper: Decide then if you wish the design balanced from the center, in alternating groups, or whatever. Uses include collars, cuffs (including those of gloves), hems, pillows, napkin rings, towels, lamp shades, etc.

Wouldn't you like to have a family remember you at mealtime? Specially designed luncheon mats are marvelous gifts. My mother gave each of us girls a piece of our maternal grandmother's trousseau linen and from my share I made place mats with appliquéd strawberry motif. The berries were cut from the material of the dinette drapes, the edges bound in a tape matching the walls in color, and somehow using these mats has let my grandmother and her love of stitchery live again.

The most personal gift you can give would be one with an individual's name or initials on it. Or his or her face could be interpreted in stitchery. Each stitchery I do has meaning beyond the object shown. A tribute to a friend, Esther, reflected her inspirational qualities as a dedicated teacher. The colors were white for pureness and holiness, blue for honesty, gold for respect and thoughtfulness. Every shape was a symbol—eternal light, house of worship, crown of David. The ways of personalizing a gift are endless. If a child has a favorite animal or toy such as a rabbit or a mobile in his room or a doll, that would make a good subject for stitchery.

If you are religious, your background may have a great influence on your life and on your stitchery. Perhaps a mural for your sanctuary would make a fine group project, as elaborate or simple as you wish. In your home, stitchery can so easily become a family affair, an activity for a get-together or party (perfect for a shower, for example), or simply contagious fun.

PART TWO

Making the Stitchery

BACKGROUND FABRIC

Of the many fabrics and materials suitable as backgrounds for stitcheries, I am partial to linen, one of the earliest fabrics used in ecclesiastical embroidery. Pure linen comes in many weaves and thicknesses. It is easy to work on and it holds its shape. It is durable, resists mildew and moths, and improves with age and washings. Even if the linen has discolored, it can be washed and bleached without falling apart. If you like the antique look, though, why not use linen as is or fill in the background with stitchery? Don't be afraid to use a yellowed piece of linen, or perhaps one that may have a few stains on it. Just remember your designs can cover the stains and the soft antique tone of linen may be just what you are looking for and ideal for your subject.

I like to shop at remnant counters and have purchased lovely linen fabrics for less than half their original price. Have you ever thought of turning to thrift stores for articles made of linen? Since many of my stitchery designs are small, I am able to use the fabric from almost any size article.

A neutral, off-white or black fabric will serve as a good background for most colors. On the list below, materials marked by asterisks do not fray or ravel when cut.

Burlap   Dishcloths
Homespun   *Leather
Decorator samples   *Felt
Towels
*Mesh bags from fruit and vegetable departments
Linen: altar, canvas, curtain, drapery, handkerchief,
    toweling
*Cotton-rayon-linen mixture, as in drapery fabric
Linen-type rayon drapery and dress fabric

THREADS, YARNS AND THEIR USES

A large selection of different kinds of thread and yarn is not a necessity for creative work, but it often can be your inspiration as well as your supply material. Start collecting skeins and scraps of yarn, string, thread, etc. and keep them in see-through plastic bags. Remember, anything white can be dyed if so desired by using commercial or homemade vegetable dyes.

Below is a list of threads and yarns that my students and I have used. If you have access to other unusual materials, do try using them. One of the bywords of creative stitchery is "Keep experimenting!"

Carpet Warp, Rug Yarn comes in different thicknesses, a variety of colors and is inexpensive. It is useful in making practice stitches and in some stitcheries.

Crewel Yarn. I have used many types of yarn in my work, but my favorite is crewel yarn. This soft, two-ply worsted, mothproof yarn is easy to work with because of its elasticity. It comes in many shades of each color. My embroidered monogram, which appears in the front of this book, was made with four shades of gold and with only one stitch, and is very effective, I think.

Crochet Thread is often used by students for couching purposes and filling in shapes.

Embroidery Floss (silk or cotton) was used to fill in the backgrounds of Daisies in the Field and Free Form designs and many other stitcheries. See color section.

Knitting Yarn (wool and synthetics) is ideal for many kinds of fabrics, especially burlap. Easy to work with. The large white daisies in Daisies in the Field (color section) were made with synthetic yarn; the shading was done with crewel yarns.

Metallic Threads are used to add highlights to a number of my designs and were used in outlining the butterflies in Daisies in the Field.

Sewing Thread (cotton, silk, nylon, linen and polyester in different thicknesses). Some of these threads were used in filling in the background of Daisies in the Field. Polyester thread was used to couch the entire crewel-yarn design of flowers and leaves in Tropical Flowers. See color.

Chenille and Decorative Yarn is too bulky to be sewn through most fabrics except coarse mesh as in bags that fruits and vegetables are sometimes packed in, but it can be attached to any background fabric with couching. Thread or yarn that *will* sew through the fabric can of course be used for any stitch. (For more information, see "Couching and the Ways to Do It.") This type yarn was used in designing Free Form design. By using these yarns, a design can be laid out in a short time, pinned in place and stitched and completed quickly.

Novelty Type Yarn. Angora and mohair are both fluffy yarns. One example of their many uses is Dandelion design, where the puff ball was made with off-white mohair yarn.

Weaving Yarn (perle cotton) was used in outlining and filling in forms of the Contour design, opposite, some places using one row of Outline and other places two to five rows down the center of the design.

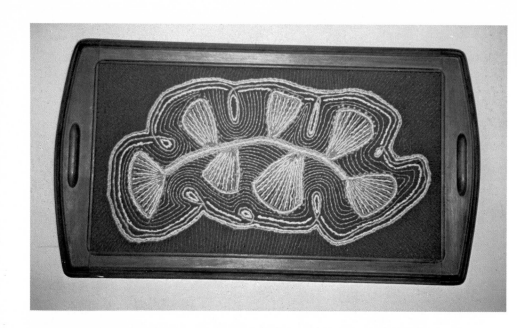

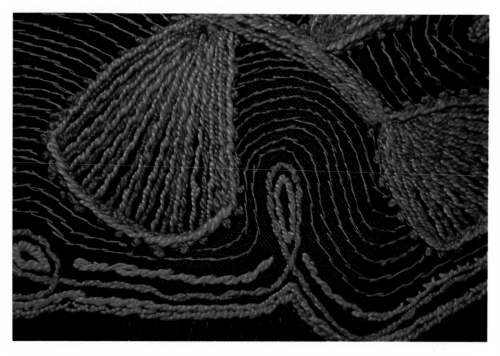

Even the basically simple free form design becomes completely different through the variety of stitchery techniques used. 14" x 25".

Ravelings from linen can be used for stitching. I needed a yellow to match the background of Free Form design for my initials. Here raveling was used with great success. Yarns can be salvaged by unraveling a knitted garment. To smooth out the yarn, wrap it around a cutting board, not too tightly. After it has been placed on the board, tuck in the end to secure it. Then dip it in cool water and let it dry. When completely dry, it can be rolled into balls and be ready for use when needed.

I have seen stitcheries that incorporated horsehair, raffia, rope (nylon, hemp and jute) in their designs, and so, to repeat, "Keep experimenting."

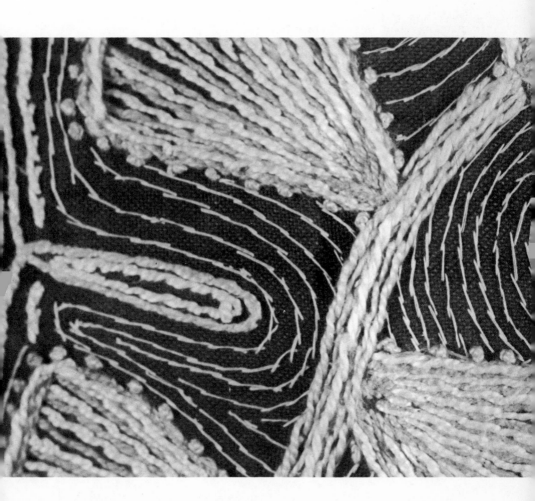

TYPES OF NEEDLES AND THEIR USES

EMBROIDERY CREWEL NEEDLE: (DARNING NEEDLE can be substituted)
Sharp point—large eye—comes in packages of assorted sizes 3–9
and 5–10.

USES   6-ply embroidery floss   Thin metallic thread
2-ply crewel yarn   Some beading
Sewing thread   All type fabrics
Crochet thread   Couching (threads)

EMBROIDERY CREWEL NEEDLE NO. 2:
Sharp point—large eye—is the same size needle as chenille
needle No. 20. Comes six in a package and is 1 ⅝ inches long.

USES   2-ply crewel yarn   Ravelings
6-ply embroidery floss   Sewing thread
Crochet thread   All type fabrics
Mohair yarn

CHENILLE NEEDLES:
Sharp point—large eye—1 ¾ inches long. Also comes in a package of assorted sizes 18–22.

USES   4-ply knitting yarn   Ravelings
2-ply perle cotton yarn   Carpet warp
Metallic thread   Burlap and other loosely
Mohair   woven fabrics
Angora

YARN NEEDLE:

      Heavy—sharp point—large eye—comes two in a package; 2 inches and 2 ¾ inches long.

USES   4-ply knitting yarns
       Heavy type yarns
       Burlap and other loosely
       woven fabrics

BEADING ASSORTMENT NEEDLES:

      Sharp point—long eye—very thin wire and comes four in a package; 1 ⅞ inches–2 ¼ inches long.

USES   Beading (small beads)
       All type fabrics

TAPESTRY NEEDLES:

      Blunt point—long eye—comes in sizes 18–22 (usually six to a package).

USES   Prevents catching fabric
       with point of needle for
       threaded Running Stitch
       in loosely woven fabrics

STITCHING HINTS

How to Cut Fabric Evenly:

Pull thread out at a point where the removed thread will make a straight line in the fabric.

Cut fabric on line made where thread was pulled out.

Keep cut edges of fabric from raveling by placing masking tape along cut edges, which comes off easily when stitchery is completed.

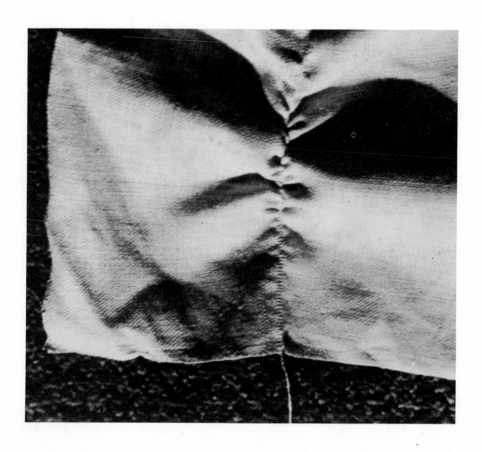

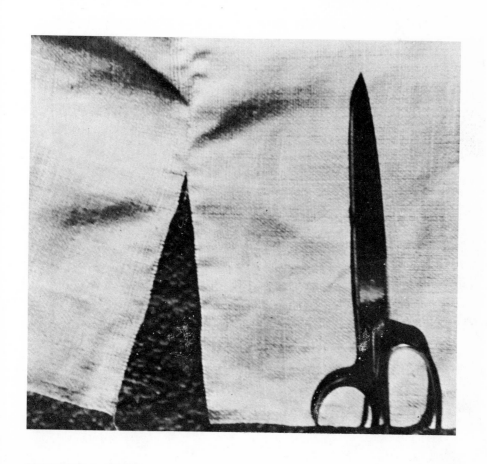

Cut thread or yarn straight across, not on an angle. Moisten in mouth and flatten cut end between teeth (unless you are doubling the thread—then it would be holding two cut ends together). The yarn will slip more easily through the eye.

If yarn is thick: Loop a piece of regular sewing thread around a piece of yarn, keeping the sewing thread doubled at the cut ends. Pull the sewing thread through the eye of the embroidery needle.

If yarn is soft and flimsy, lacking body: Cut yarn straight and pull it across a piece of beeswax or candle. This will stiffen the yarn to allow it to be pulled more easily through the needle's eye.

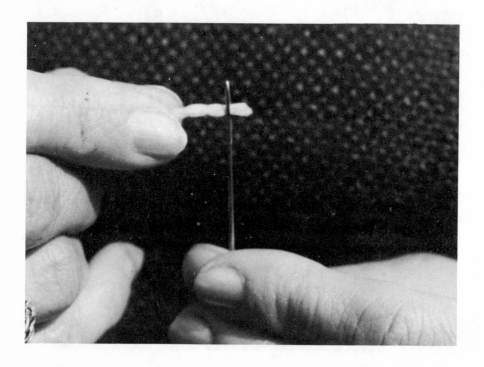

Making a Knot

Moisten forefinger and wrap yarn around it one time only. Roll yarn off the finger with your thumb. Use middle finger to pull the loop down, which will make a small knot at the end of the yarn. (If you are working with yarn or thread doubled, both ends should be knotted together by the same method as above.) Note that a few short stitches can be made in the beginning in place of a knot, and some people feel this is the more "professional" approach to stitchery.

Do Not Make Stitches Too Tight

The background fabric will draw up and your work will lose its shape if stitches are too tight. Background should remain flat at all times. If you desire, a hoop can be used to hold a stitchery taut while in progress.

All is not lost should your background have a slightly puckered look. Here is one suggestion to correct that mistake and salvage your work: If you have enough space left on the outer margin of your piece, the design could be padded on the back side with pieces of old nylon stockings (or quilt padding), tacking down the padding by taking a few stitches into nylon pieces and background fabric (take care not to let these stitches go through to the right side). Then you will have a two-dimensional design and it can be finished the way you had planned, as a framed picture or as a collage for a tote bag or such.

When to Stop

When length of yarn is around three inches it is time to stop and take at least three short stitches, one on top of the other, on the back side before cutting away excess yarn. This too prevents tangles and unnecessary bulk on the back of the stitchery—and also keeps work from ripping in the process of washing, steam pressing and framing.

If you need to finish off with a short end of thread or yarn: Place the needle in the fabric with only the eye showing. Thread the needle with that bit of yarn remaining and pull it through to the other side of the fabric. Remember, make at least three more stitches on the back side of your stitchery, one on top of the other, to keep work from pulling out.

To keep from losing a threaded needle in work, wrap the excess thread around top and bottom of needle, when you are not working on stitchery.

KEEPING YARN IN ORDER

Pull yarn from center of skein to prevent tangling. The length of yarn can be approximately thirty-six inches; if it is too long, it twists and tangles while stitching. (If this does happen, let threaded needle dangle to unwind itself.)

To keep a ball of yarn from unwinding and getting tangled, a small piece of Scotch or masking tape can be used to hold the cut end down to the ball. It really saves aggravation and time.

Scraps of yarn can be tied together in color families; you may find a need for a certain color to add contrast of color or you may need only a small bit to finish your work. I have also made two stitcheries from such scraps of yarn, Weeping Willow and Autumn Burning Bush. Keep two bundles, one for short and another for long pieces of yarn.

A DICTIONARY OF STITCHES

There are over two hundred variations of stitches, but in creating the designs in this book only six basic ones were employed, with several variations. As you stitch along to become familiar with a few you approach the time of experimentation. The joy of painting with a needle is being free to do some exploring on your own. It is an enormous satisfaction knowing a stitchery was your idea and not one that someone else created for you to copy. What you do does not have to be perfect. Strangely enough, if it does satisfy you, it usually satisfies—and pleases—others. It's like doodling. If you once get started, you'll never want to stop.

It takes practice to be an expert typist or to be able to play the piano, and the same thing is true about stitching. Once I knew no more than some of you about the techniques and possibilities of embroidery, but having made clothes, I had learned a few basic stitches and could apply them in creating stitcheries. The Outline Stitch, for example, so often used in designs was what I used putting in hems.

Just as an artist experiments with colors on his palette before he applies them to canvas, we all need to practice making stitches for their own sake before we can express our visions. My first practice stitches were made on decorators' sample swatches, all the same size fabric. After completing several, I mounted each one on cardboard and they have been useful in teaching variations and combinations of stitches as well as colors. Or practice on a checked kitchen towel, using one color yarn. Hem it, have a dowel rod run through, and it can be hung. (See "Displaying a Stitchery.") The artist keeps a sketchbook of ideas which he can refer to. Your sampler serves the same purpose.

Practice making stitches on any type fabric, plain, striped or checkered. Stitches can vary in size. Stitches can go in any direction, up, down and across. They can be made in rows, alone, in groups and in varying distances from one another. (See also "Discovering Designs.") Even though you may have practiced on your sampler long and well, it is still advisable to keep a piece of fabric close at hand, as "scratch pad" while working on your stitchery. You might like to try some variation of the stitch you had planned.

There are many uses for a sampler; it can be mounted and framed, or it can be stapled to paper and placed in a notebook of ideas. I like using Kleer Vu page protectors, the kind that have a black sheet of paper between a folded sheet of plastic, which can be kept in a binder. The static of the plastic keeps everything in place without staples or glue. Pencil sketches of ideas for future stitcheries go here, too. Or you can make some useful object of your sampler—pin cushion, pot holder, eyeglass case, purse or decorative pocket, or other examples. Why not practice making stitches down the seams of your jeans or your child's T-shirt.

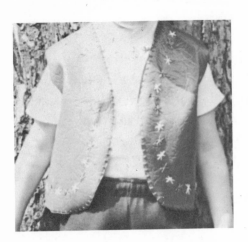

Do not worry if your stitches (even the Chain Stitch) are not uniform in size. A stitch can be made small or large or graduate in size. The size of the stitches will depend partially upon the thickness of yarn, or thinness of thread and the type background fabric you are using.

As you become familiar and learn how to make different stitches, you will discover that most stitches are related. The yarn must be held under the point of the needle in making a Loop Stitch, regardless of the name attached to the stitch.

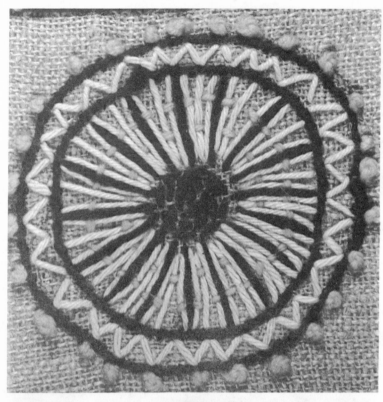

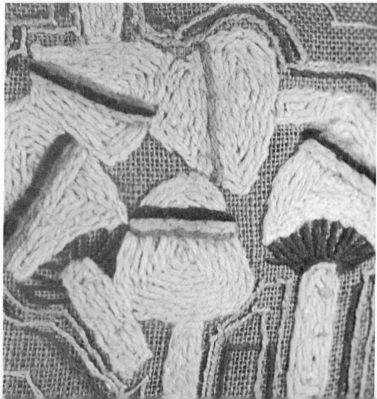

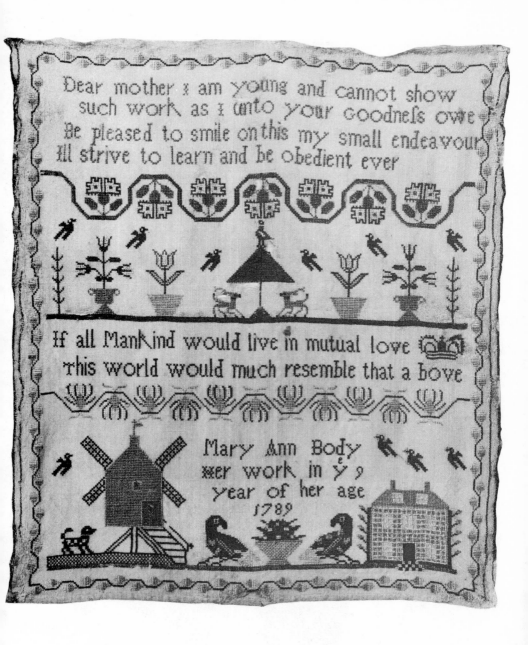

Dear mother I am young and cannot show
such work as I unto your Goodnefs owe
Be pleased to smile on this my small endeavour
Ill strive to learn and be obedient ever

If all Mankind would live in mutual love
This world would much resemble that a bove

Mary Ann Body
her work in y⁹
year of her age
1789

The two examples opposite prepared by my students show how
the samplers of creative stitchery now have many forms in contrast to the quaint example above. *Credit: Victoria and Albert
Museum. Crown Copyright*

MAKING THE STITCHERY

THE OUTLINE STITCH

This stitch is easy to do and is versatile; I have used it in most of my stitcheries, both as "single column" to define an area or indicate a thin line, or in rows close together to provide the effect of a thick, solid area. Note the stem opposite. Thickness can be varied by the length and width of the stitch itself, too. The Outline Stitch makes an unbroken line, as you see in these illustrations.

The yarn should be held loosely above or below the needle. Both ways are correct, only the slant will be different. Try making a few stitches both ways, then decide on the preferable slant. Seven stitches to the inch were the average number used in the designs pictured in this book, although they can be made smaller or larger, depending on the intended effect.

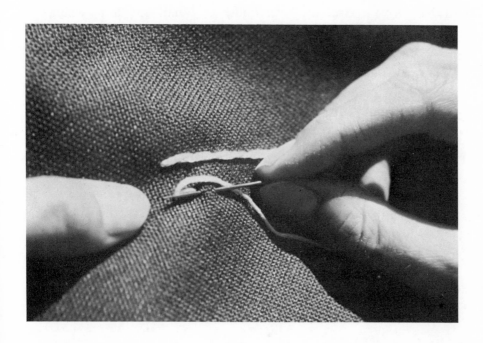

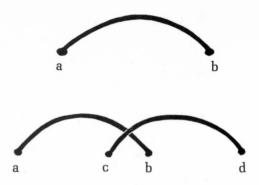

Steps in Making the Outline Stitch

Start with yarn on back side of fabric. Bring needle through at *a* on top side. Hold yarn above the needle and make a stitch between *a* and *b*, which would be from *left to right*, the usual direction of this stitch.

Bring the needle back under at *b* and out at *c*, which is closely left of *b*. So you are going *right to left*.

Make the next stitch on top of fabric from *c* to *d*, going *left to right*.

Continue as many times as needed, first bringing the needle back under from *d* and making next stitch on top of fabric, as you did from *c* to *d*, etc. (The left-handed person would make the stitch just the opposite, backward.)

When going around a curve, make the stitches loose and somewhat smaller to keep the background fabric from drawing up and losing its shape. For a corded effect, the stitches should be made close together and short. This corded stitch was used as a Couching Stitch to attach the lines of yarn in the center of each loop of the Free Form design. The yarn was held above the needle.

The Outline Stitch was used also in the Contour design,

varying from one row of stitches to five rows in the center of the design. The detail of the Free Form design below shows a use of Outline to fill in—to constitute—the design. It is especially appropriate for monograms and names.

RUNNING STITCHES

The Running Stitch is also the Basting Stitch one uses in sewing. It is one of the easiest stitches to learn and makes a good basic stitch for many decorative stitches. The Running Stitch can be used for filling in space, outlining, couching flowers, stars, etc. It can be made to go in any direction, in rows, groups, singly, far apart, close together, and can even cross itself (Cross Stitch). The stitches can all be made the same size, vary in size and alternate in size (big, little, big, etc.). Once you have mastered the Running Stitch, the possibilities are endless.

Short Running Stitches, made with crewel yarn, averaging six stitches to an inch, were used in outlining the cattails of the Cattails design. A short Running Stitch is used to secure loops of detached Chain Stitch and other variations of the Chain Stitch. It was used to secure the Bundle Stitch.

Medium-size Running Stitches, made with crewel yarn, averaging two stitches to an inch, were used in couching the decorative (heavy) yarn to background fabric in the Free Form design.

b   a   d   c   b   a

STEPS IN MAKING A STRAIGHT RUNNING STITCH

Thread needle and don't forget the knot. Start with yarn on back side of fabric. Bring needle through at *a* and make a Running Stitch between *a* and *b*. With needle at *b* on back side, bring it over to *c* on back side and then bring it out to *c* on top side. Make another Running Stitch on top side between *c* and *d*. Repeat steps *a* through *d* as many times as needed to fill the space.

     MAKING THE STITCHERY

Steps in Making a Single (Ubroken) Line Running Stitch

Make a row of Running Stitches. Come back and make a row of Running Stitches in between each stitch made with the same color yarn, for outlining and to fill in space.

A different color can be used for the second row of stitches made in between the first row of Running Stitches.

Steps in Making the Long Running Stitch

Long Running Stitches were used to fill in the open shapes of the Free Form design. The Outline Stitch was used to couch (secure) the long Running Stitch to the background fabric. Various lengths of long Running Stitches were loosely sewn to follow the contour of each shape. They were spaced on the average of one-half inch apart at one end and gradually came closer together until they touched in some places. Stitch can start at top or bottom.

Start with needle on back side of fabric and bring it through at *a* on top side. Make a long Running Stitch between *a* and *b*.

With needle at *b* on back side, bring it through at *c* on top side and make another Running Stitch between *c* and *d*. Make as many long Running Stitches as needed to fill each open shape.

Satin-Type Running Stitch are Running Stitches that are made close together, almost a covered look. This stitch is ideal for filling in leaves as was done in the Dandelion design. It can be used for making flower petals and by using the long and short Running Stitch, they could be shaded (from light to dark colors). The legs and feet of the Winter Bird design were made with this stitch.

Start with needle on back side of fabric. Bring it through at *a* on top side and make a Running Stitch between *a* and *b*.

With needle at *b* on back side, bring it over (on back side) a bit to the left of *b* at *c* and make a tiny Running Stitch on the back side between *b* and *c*. Bring needle out at *c* to top side and make a Running Stitch between *c* and *d*. With needle at *d* (on back side) make a tiny Running Stitch between *d* and next stitch, as you did between *b* and *c*. Bring needle through to top side and repeat steps *a* through *d* as many times as needed to fill the space with the satin-type Running Stitch.

Long and Short Running Stitches. These stitches give you the opportunity to practice doodling. So many combinations and variations can be made for accent of color contrast (shading) and interest to a stitchery.

Uses of Running Stitches include wave and leaf motifs, brick patterns, border designs and background patterns.

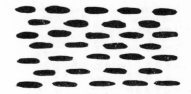

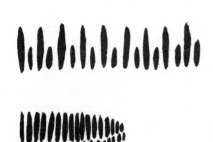

Checkerboard Pattern with Running Stitches. One color crewel yarn was used, averaging ten Running Stitches to each group in making the background for The Weaver design. The important thing to remember is to use the same number and same length of stitches in each group, so that each block will be the same size.

Two colors can be used in making the checkerboard pattern. When completed, for added color and interest, some embroidery could be planned for each block or in just a few blocks. This makes a very nice background for a pillow top and is easy to plan. The pattern can be worked on paper first. Two shades of one color can be used for this type background.

STEPS IN MAKING RUNNING STITCHES MEETING AT ONE POINT

Running Stitches Meeting at One Point were used in making the tiny orange flowers in the Cattails design. Although three stitches were used in this particular design, the number of Running Stitches and size (length) can vary. An example of this was used in making the sprouts on the stems and the roots of the plant in the Ivy Vine design. Star and flower designs can be worked with this type stitch; used for texture on tree trunks.

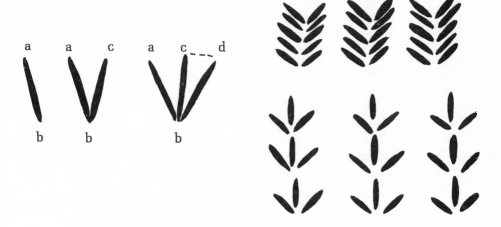

Start with needle on back side of fabric and bring it through at *a* on top side. Make a Running Stitch between *a* and *b*.

With needle on back side at *b*, on back side bring it out *close* to *b* (making a *tiny* Running Stitch). Make another Running Stitch between *b* and *c* on top side of fabric.

With needle on back side at *c*, bring it over on the back side to *d* (making a Running Stitch between *c* and *d*). Bring needle through at *d* on top side and make a Running Stitch between *d* and *b*.

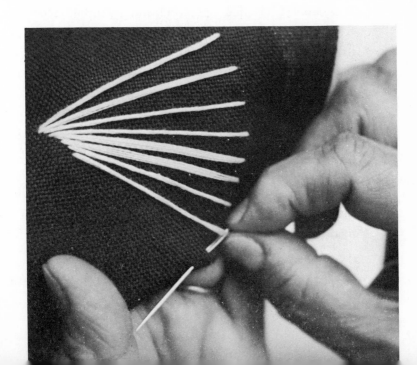

VARIATIONS OF THE RUNNING STITCH

THREADED RUNNING STITCH

This is a fun way of creating different and interesting patterns. It can be used to symbolize waves, clouds, stones, mountains, roofs, braid effects, etc. Think of different ways you can use the single Threaded Running Stitch. It can also be used to fill in space and to add texture to a design.

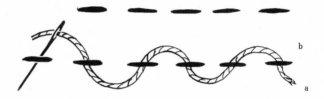

STEPS IN MAKING THE THREADED RUNNING STITCH (SINGLE THREAD)

Make a row of Running Stitches, leaving the same amount of space between each stitch.

With a contrasting color of yarn, bring needle through at *a* from back side of fabric and go up under the first Running Stitch, then down under the second Running Stitch. Repeat going up under the next stitch and down under the next one until you have gone through all the Running Stitches made. *Remember:* Each threaded stitch is left loose and not sewn to the fabric. You can adjust the size loop you wish to make. If you decide on a large one, it will probably have to be secured with a stitch to hold it in place. Experiment. It's fun to make your own discoveries. When finished going through all the Running Stitches, to prevent the threaded stitch from pulling out, secure it with at least three small stitches one on top of another on back side of fabric.

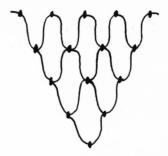

Threaded Running Stitch (Double)

After completing the single Threaded Running Stitches, bring needle through with same color yarn from back side at *b* and go down under the first Running Stitch and up under the second stitch, etc., until you have gone through all the Running Stitches that had been threaded.

Rows of Running Stitches can alternate for the threaded stitch, which gives you a netting type effect and can be incorporated nicely if making a roof, texture, a net, etc.

Steps in Making the Bundle Stitch

Bundle Stitch was used in filling in spaces in The Castle design. As a beginner, start with a specified amount of Running Stitches. It is a natural way to symbolize hay stacks.

Make a group of three or more long vertical Running Stitches, leaving a small amount of space between stitches.

Bring needle through from back side and make a small Running Stitch around the center of the group, pulling the long vertical stitches together to make a Bundle Stitch. Repeat as many times as needed to fill the space. End each Bundle with at least three small Running Stitches one on top of the other on the back side.

THE HERRINGBONE STITCH

This is sometimes called the Catch Stitch. It is easy to learn and covers a great deal of space without using too much yarn. It can be used as a background stitch for other stitches. The stitches can be made close together, far apart, and graduate in size, narrow to wide and vice versa. The Herringbone Stitch is made up of Running Stitches that cross at top and bottom, resembling overlapping tepees. Stitches made with crewel yarn averaged six to the inch for designs used in this book. It can be used for texture, contrast, etc. The Herringbone Stitch in different sizes and colors was used exclusively in creating the mountains in the Harvest design. The Herringbone Stitch was used to fill in the shapes of the leaves of the Ivy Vine design and the leaves of the Strawberry design. In creating the City Abstract design, the Herringbone Stitch was made between two parallel lines, and it was used as a background for other stitches in The Gladiator, Traffic Lights and other designs.

Green and Blue Maze, here areas of Herringbone Stitch are defined and accented by the Outline Stitch.

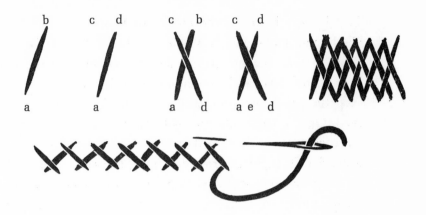

STEPS IN MAKING THE HERRINGBONE STITCH

Start with needle on back side of fabric and bring it through at *a* on top side. Make a Running Stitch between *a* and *b*.

With needle at *b* on back side, bring it over to the left of *b* at *c* and make a Running Stitch between *b* and *c*.

Bring needle through at *c* to top side and make a Running Stitch between *c* and *d*, crossing over the Running Stitch previously made between *a* and *b*.

Repeat steps *a*, *b*, *c* and *d* as many times as it takes to fill in the space.

THE CHAIN STITCH

This is thought to be the oldest stitch made. It is a Loop Stitch and looks like a single crochet stitch. I like the Chain Stitch, because it has many uses and I have used it in many designs. It resembles a chain of links, and to keep the appearance, the stitches should be made loose and even. On the back side you will discover a Running Stitch for each Chain Stitch made on the top side. It is easy to work the Chain Stitch around corners, because it is a flexible stitch. It can be used in creating an entire design, for outlining, filling in space, combined with other stitches, for leaves, flowers, monograms, texture, bark on· trees, and as a Couching Stitch. The detail of Harvest shows the texture of a built-up variation of the chain.

The size stitch to make will be your decision. The thickness of yarn used will also be a factor.

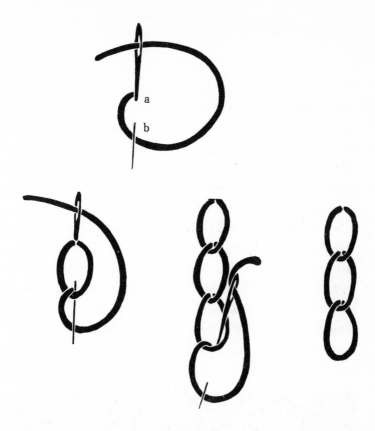

Steps in Making the Chain Stitch

Start with needle on back side of fabric. Bring it through at *a* on top side. Hold yarn with left thumb (right-handed person), the length stitch you plan to make. Insert needle at *a* or close to it and bring it through at *b* while holding yarn under the point of the needle. This will make a Loop Stitch (Chain Stitch).

To continue making more Loop Stitches for the Chain, hold yarn at *b*, length of stitch, with thumb and insert needle to the right of *b*, which will keep chain from twisting.

Repeat steps *a* and *b* as many times as needed.

VARIATIONS OF THE CHAIN STITCH

Detached Chain Stitch is exactly what the name implies. This, too, is a Loop Stitch and is sometimes called the Lazy Daisy Stitch. Each stitch is made separately and to hold it in place, a small Running Stitch is made at the bottom of each loop. The stitches can all be made the same size or various sizes and can be used singly in rows or in groups.

The Detached Chain Stitch was used in groups for the flower petals of the Dandelion design. It was used singly for the flowers in the background of Daisies in the Field, a detail of which is shown in color. Also in the color section is Springtime; there the Detached Chain Stitch was used in rows for the flowers and leaves.

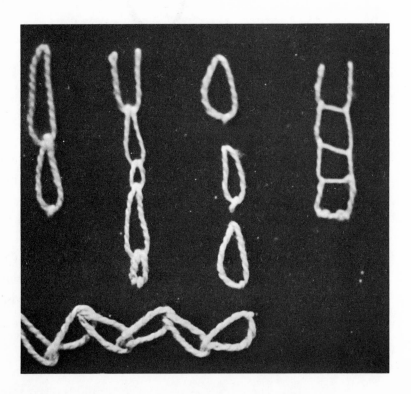

Start with needle on back side of fabric. Bring it through at *a* on top side. Hold yarn at *b* (with thumb) and insert needle at *a* or close to it and bring it through at *b*, while keeping yarn under the point of the needle. This will make one Loop Stitch, or single-link Chain Stitch. With needle at *b* on top side, make a small Running Stitch. This will hold each loop in place. The same steps are used each time a Detached Chain Stitch is made.

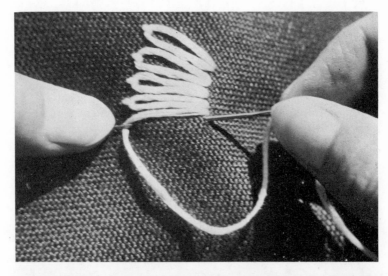

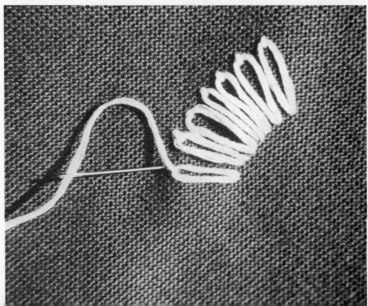

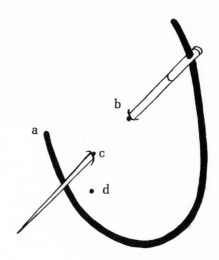

Steps in Making the Open Chain Stitch

Open Chain Stitch (Fly Stitch) is similar to the Detached Chain Stitch. Instead of making the Chain Stitch closed, this stitch is left wide open. When the bottom of the loop has been secured with a Running Stitch, it seems to take the shape of a V or to symbolize a bird flying. This stitch can be arranged in groups or singly. With a little practice, it is the type stitch that has many possibilities. It can be used for fill-in in space, texture, flowers, feathers and tree trunks. You may discover other ways in making use of this stitch.

Start with needle on back side of fabric. Bring it through at *a* on top side. Hold yarn at *b* with thumb and insert needle at *c*. Bring needle through at *b*. This makes one Open Chain Stitch.

With needle at *b* on top side, make a small Running Stitch between *b* and *d* to hold the loop of the Open Chain Stitch in place. To secure the stitch, if you are making only one, don't forget to take three tiny stitches on back side between *b* and *d* before cutting away excess yarn.

SINGLE FEATHER STITCH

Basically, it is a Loop Stitch and similar to the Blanket and Buttonhole Stitch. It is made vertically (top to bottom) but the Blanket Stitch is made horizontally (left to right, side to side crosswise). The single Feather Stitch can be uniform in size, vary in size, close together or far apart. This is a versatile stitch and can be used for many things in a stitchery such as feathers, texture, tree bark, vines, etc. Various sizes of the Feather Stitch were used to symbolize vines growing between each cattail in the Cattails design. It was also used to fill in the background of Daisies in the Field design in color. Experiment! Try making double Feather Stitches.

The variations of the single Feather Stitch, also known as the Blanket Stitch, can be used for waves, feathers, leaves, as well as borders and attaching appliqué.

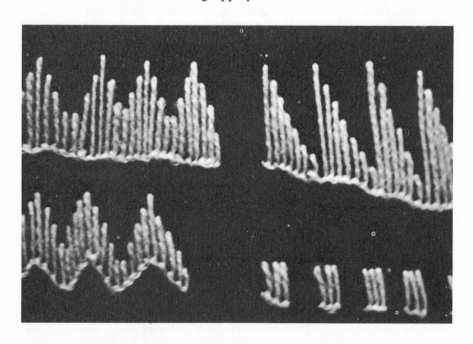

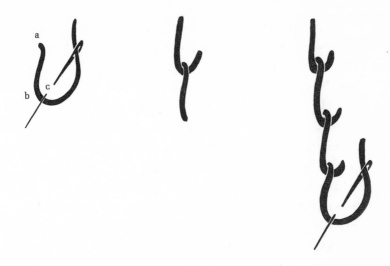

STEPS IN MAKING THE SINGLE FEATHER STITCH

Start with yarn on back side of fabric. Bring needle through at *a* and hold yarn down with thumb at *b*, length of stitch to be made. Insert needle at *c* on top side, while holding yarn under point of the needle, to make the loop at the bottom of each Feather Stitch.

Hold yarn with thumb at *b*, length of stitch to be made, and repeat steps *b* and *c* for each connecting stitch you plan to make.

FRENCH KNOTS

French Knots may take a bit longer to learn how to make, because there are two important steps to each stitch. One thing to remember is not to wrap the yarn (coils) too tightly around the needle, or they will be difficult to slip off. The second thing to remember is to insert the needle close to the spot where the needle came through. If needle is inserted in the same hole, the coils will be pulled through to the back side and you will have lost your French Knot. The size knot will depend upon the number of times the yarn is wrapped around the needle and the thickness of the yarn. French Knots can be used for a beaded effect, bubbles, flower centers, texture, in groups, singly, and combined with other stitches. When the knots are worked closely together, the pattern is called "candlewicking." Note the effect of French Knots in The Olive Tree. French Knots were used in filling in the Cattails design for a textured effect, and were combined with tiny Running Stitches in making the centers of the flowers in Tropical Flowers design.

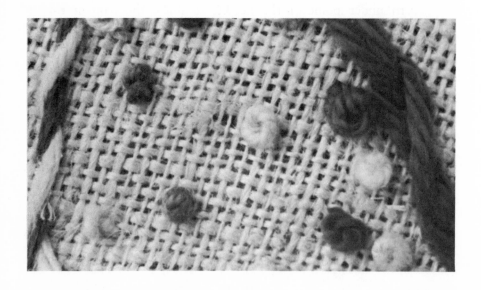

Steps in Making French Knots

Start with yarn on back side. Bring needle through at *a* on top side. Hold yarn down with your left thumb. Wrap yarn around needle a few times, close to the tip. Hold coils on needle while moving it back close to your starting point.

Insert needle at *b*, carefully holding the wrapped coils with your thumb, so that they remain on top when needle is pulled through to back side of fabric. Make a stitch (tiny Running) on back side to secure (French Knot).

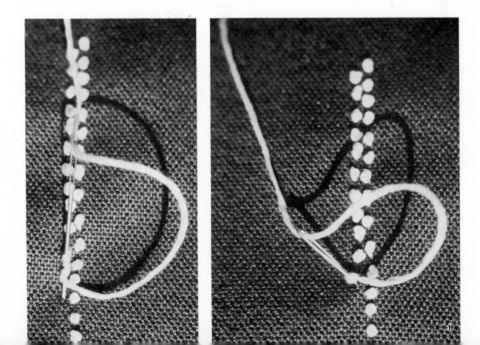

CITY ABSTRACT DESIGN

After the areas were marked off on the background fabric (paper patterns can be used), the Herringbone Stitch was done in two directions and three shades: light blue, a; medium blue, b; medium green, c. Alternate color combinations are: orange and rust; cherry red and pink; lime green and aqua or turquoise; orange and pink. The Herringbone is really used as a background stitch. The added Outline gives texture and defines the areas.

STRAWBERRY DESIGN

After Outline Stitches in red,
French Knots in a light green
added the needed texture
and color contrast; the leaves,
of course, are Herringbone
Stitch.

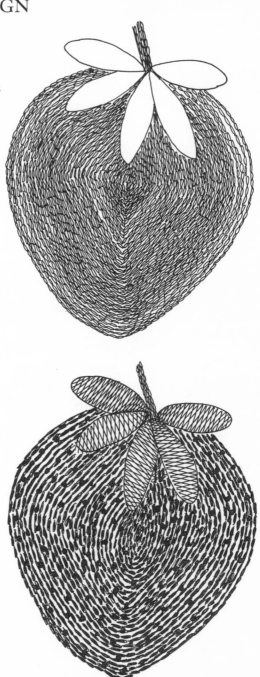

IVY VINE DESIGN

The ivy vine is a fairly hardy and attractive plant. Its leaves are shiny and waxy, and it is considered an evergreen shrub. This plant has a tendency to cling to smooth surfaces with fine roots on its stems. It is a familiar ground and wall covering and is often used as a house plant.

I had taken some close-up pictures of ivy and decided it would be a good subject to sketch and use for a stitchery. It symbolizes long life and that was good enough for me.

I was lucky to find an old frame, which was an ideal size for the design. Off-white altar linen was purchased at the remnant counter in one of the department stores. The linen was cut to fit the frame. Then masking tape was used on all sides to prevent it from raveling.

The design was drawn directly onto the background fabric with a pencil, starting with an S curve line in the center for the stem. Having studied the natural growth system, I allowed space for the design to grow; that was to add more stems, leaves and roots.

SUPPLIES

    1 crewel embroidery needle
    2 pair scissors: long pointed; to cut fabric
                 short pointed; to cut yarn
    1 9½- by 20-inch piece of off-white altar linen
    1 pencil; soft lead for sketching
    Paper
    1 roll masking tape, ¾ inch wide
    1 skein of each shade, 100 per cent 2-ply wool crewel
       yarn; medium green and light green

1 old frame 10½ by 21 inches, 1 inch wide
1 small can liquid sander
1 small jar gold metal enamel
1 small jar each gold and silver metal enamel
1 small can turpentine
Empty can
Rags
Newspapers
2 paintbrushes

Size of framed design
10½ by 21 inches

Size of design
5 by 14½ inches

After the design was transferred to the background, medium green Herringbone Stitches were used for all leaves. One, two and three rows of light green Outline Stitches were used respectively for veins, short stems and the long curved stem, which then branches out into single rows of Outline for the main part of the roots.

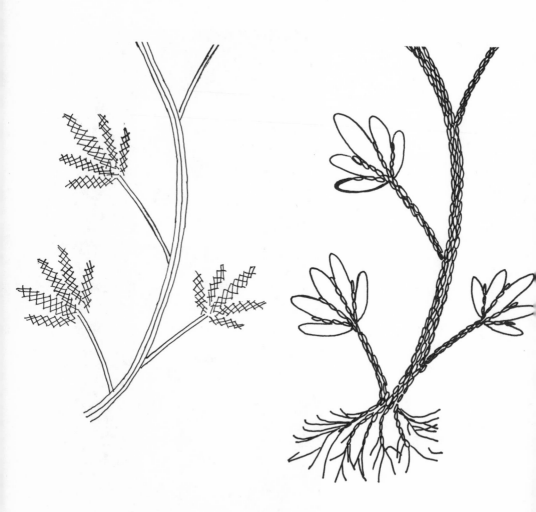

MAKING THE STITCHERY

Light green Running Stitches were used for all sprouts and the finer roots. Alternate color combinations are: shaded reds and greens on white background; reverse forest green background fabric with white.

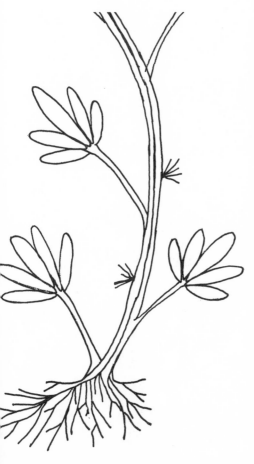

DANDELION DESIGN

Below left: Light green satin-type Running Stitch used to fill in all leaves.

Below right: Medium green Outline Stitches used to outline leaves; light green Outline Stitches used in three rows for stems and singly for the two oval buds; off-white Outline Stitches are used for the two bud sprouts and for the large center flower.

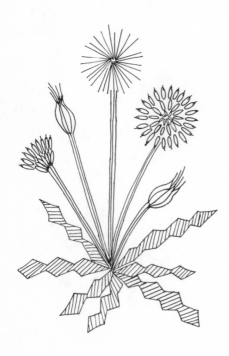

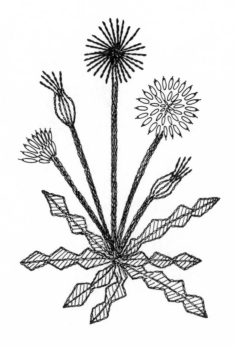

MAKING THE STITCHERY

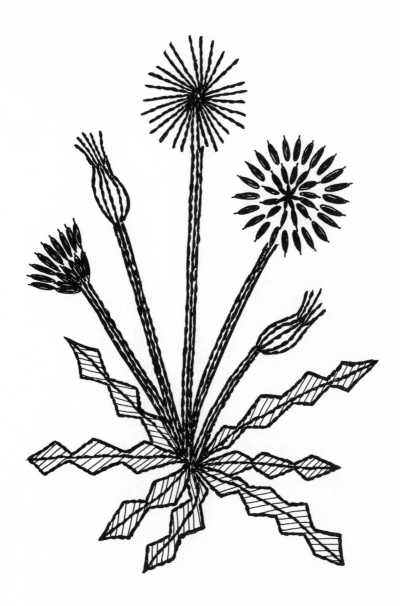

Medium orange Detached Chain Stitches for the very center of
the flower on the right and for the bottom of the side-view
blossom, extreme left; light orange Detached Chain Stitches for
top of the side-view blossom and for the two outer circles of the
one on the right. Alternate color combinations are: blue flowers
rather than gold on matching mat; black-eyed Susan; mums.

CATTAILS DESIGN

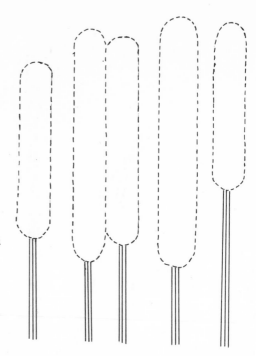

Short Running Stitches for each cattail, light rust for the first and fifth, medium rust for the second and fourth and darker shade for the middle.

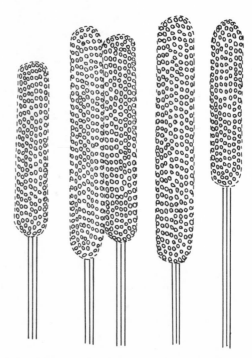

French Knots fill in each cattail using the same color scheme as before.

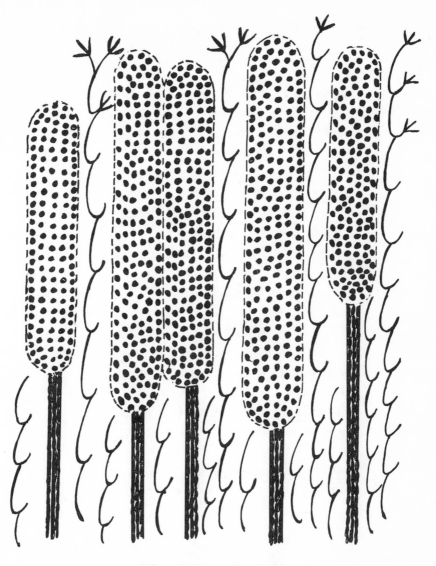

Outline Stitches in three rows for each stem, medium rust for the first, third, and fifth cattails, light rust for the second and fourth. Alternate color combinations are: shades of brown rather than rust on light beige fabric; cocoa color mat with tones of rusts and browns. Long single Feather Stitches for all the vines in the background, alternating light and medium greens. At the tops, Running Stitches radiating from one point finish the vine off in a light orange thread.

COUCHING AND THE WAYS TO DO IT

Couching is attaching or sewing fabric (as in a collage), loose threads, yarn, braid, shells and other things to create texture on a stitchery. You may have a small bit of something which would add interest to your stitchery. Yarns that cannot be sewn through fabric can be used by Couching. Laying out a design with yarn (see below) gives one the opportunity to see what type design is evolving, and it is a great way for beginners to see progress. Children especially love it. This technique is the basis of the Free Form design, which follows.

Many types of stitches and affixing thread can be used—as long as they can pass through the fabric easily; a thread or even yarn is suitable for couching.

Note that if you are working with thick yarns that ravel when cut, it is important that the loose ends be tucked under or sewn down securely for a finished look. Unless you want the loose ends left loose for effect.

Couching long Running Stitches with Outline Stitches fills in each loop of the Free Form design.

Chain, Outline, Running Stitches, French Knots, Herringbone, and Feather Stitches may all be used for couching.

I have given a number of ideas for texture in the following pages. One of the easiest and fastest stitches for me has been the Running Stitch; for couching, Outline, Herringbone and Chain Stitch work well too.

FREE FORM DESIGN

Size of framed design   13½ by 21½ inches
Size of design   7 by 15 inches

The shapes in this Free Form design could symbolize many things, depending upon the person's past experiences. One who has been to the seashore may say they look like shells. The outdoor type and one interested in birds or insects may think they represent butterflies or birds in flight. Still another, who happens to live where there is a change of seasons, may say they remind him of autumn leaves. Then there are some who will only see a few curved and straight lines, others, a fan dancer.

SUPPLIES USED IN CREATING THE FREE FORM DESIGN:

    1 crewel embroidery needle
    2 pair scissors: long pointed; to cut fabric
                     short pointed; to cut yarn
    1 12- by 20-inch piece of brown basket-weave fabric
    1 package thick gold decorative yarn
    1 skein of each color 100 per cent 2-ply wool crewel yarn:
        light gold, medium orange and dark orange
    1 small package dressmaker's straight pins
    1 roll masking tape, ¾ inch wide
    1 can Scotchgard fabric spray
    1 sponge
    2 small terry bath towels
    1 See-Thru-Steam-Thru press cloth
    Iron and ironing board
    1 unfinished frame, 12 by 20 inches, 1 inch wide

1 tube burnt umber color in oil (small size)
1 can turpentine
1 small can satin-finish varnish
1 small can wood sealer
1 sheet medium sandpaper
2 small brushes ½ inch wide
1 empty can
1 teaspoon
Rags
Newspapers

After cutting the background fabric, masking tape was placed on all sides to prevent it from raveling.

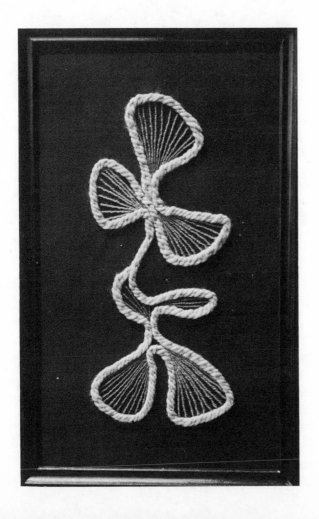

Running Stitches in medium gold-colored thread were used to subtly couch the thick yarn of the same color, which had been arranged in loops on the background fabric. Alternating color combinations are: brown fabric with light aqua and deeper shades of aqua; light-color background with any combination of colors; black fabric with white, gray and silver yarn.

I let the thick gold color yarn fall casually from my hand onto the brown background fabric, forming large swirls. After a few changes were made to create a more interesting design, I knew it was time to proceed to secure the design.

To secure the yarn design, prior to stitching, the yarn was taped to the background fabric an inch apart.

A gold color crewel yarn was used in making Running Stitches, averaging two stitches to an inch; to couch, hold the thick gold yarn to the brown background fabric.

The medium-orange crewel yarn was used to fill in the

three open forms with *loose* long Running Stitches, varying in size. The three remaining open forms were filled in with the dark orange crewel yarn with *loose* long Running Stitches, varying in size. At intervals to check a possible tautness in fabric and yarn, it was laid out on a flat surface.

The Outline Stitch was used to couch (attach) the long Running Stitches to the brown background fabric. They were made close together to give a corded effect. Medium orange color crewel yarn was used to couch the medium orange Running Stitches and the dark orange crewel yarn was used to couch the dark orange Running Stitches to the background fabric.

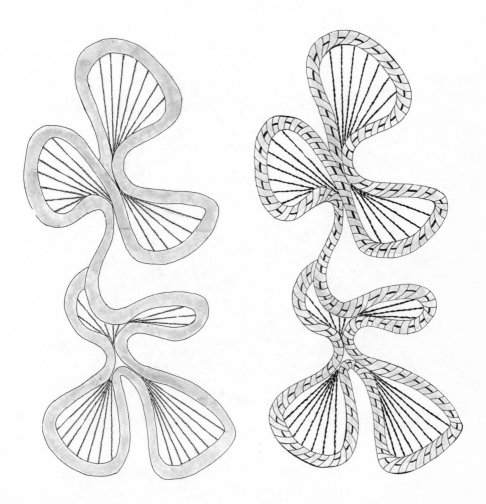

EXPLORING WAYS TO ADD INTEREST OR ACCENT

There are a number of ways to give a stitchery interest and eye appeal. Not all of the techniques have to be incorporated into one piece. But try laying a contrasting color on top of your work, or try a different type stitch, or make the same stitch loose and open enough so that the color or colors beneath will show through. These two illustrations of students' work show couching, Cross Stitch and Outline, the latter stitchery incorporating beads to fill in this Free Form design. Stitcheries mentioned in the following pages are shown earlier.

Texture and subject are nicely wedded in this stitchery.

Loops of yarn held in place with tiny Running Stitches are great for bird designs, poodles and anything requiring built-up texture. This variation of the Running Stitch can be used. If you want to keep all the loops the same size, cut a piece of cardboard and wrap each loop around the cardboard before attaching it to the fabric. Again, look closely at what you are planning to make. Look at pictures in science books or elsewhere to see what texture could be used to symbolize the object in your work. Don't leave a stone unturned. Try anything and everything. If you are not satisfied, do a little ripping.

The Tropical Flowers (see color section) design originally showed a number of flowers covered with large, loose, open Running Stitches in gold. I was thinking of the cobwebs you sometimes see in warm humid climates. But when one of my students said it gave her the feeling of being enclosed in a web, that was all I needed to hear, and that night and many more to follow I did my share of ripping. Now it is one of my favorite stitcheries. I used three shades of green for the oversize leaves; using the long Running Stitch first, and on top to couch it down to background fabric, I used polyester sewing thread on one side in the same green as the leaf but on the other side in a lighter shade of green crewel yarn, with the Outline Stitch to give it a textured look. The flowers were made with three shades of coral, using the Running Stitch graduating in size and couched with one shade of coral polyester sewing thread, using a small Running Stitch. I love the center of each flower. It is a circle of off-white French Knots that really adds texture, with small Running Stitches following the round shape in two shades of orange and one shade of pale green. Crewel yarn was used for the entire stitchery, except for the polyester thread for couching.

The Big Blue Owl design is an almost abstract form, with

exaggerated head and eyes for interest. Only three types of stitches were used to create this stitchery, but the concentration of color in certain areas and the closeness of the small Running Stitch to fill in the greater part of the bird are what make it unusual. For contrast in color, the top of the head was worked in a pattern design (Running Stitches) —three rows of dark blue with one row of yellow green. The bright orange bill and feet add contrast to the blue and yellow green. What adds much to the piece is the use of yellow green Herringbone Stitch under an open Herringbone Stitch of dark blue.

In the Cattails design, French Knots in three shades of rust add not only texture but accents of color. The green single Feather Stitch used to symbolize vines and little orange flowers in the Running Stitch add much contrast.

The Free Form design certainly shows different textures through different types of yarn and the dark brown background fabric is quite a contrast to the heavy gold color yarn. Further accent was gained through use of two shades of orange crewel yarn to fill in the spaces.

My first Dandelion stitchery was simpler than the design shown in this book and the texture of the puff ball was different. I used brown crewel yarn, making large French Knots for the seeds, and off-white mohair over it for that part which gives the ball-like shape.

Look again at the Lazy "K" Teapot design. I used light green, pale yellow, off-white and orange crewel yarns in creating this design. The letter "K" was the inspiration, as you know. It was a beginning stitchery and at the time I was using only letters of the alphabet. It is amazing how many distinct designs start in this manner. After making the letter, I drew an oval line which enclosed the K. Then I realized that it formed three triangles and a half circle to be filled in. I didn't want to lose the shape of the K so

I used off white in the four open areas. I needed a contrast in color, so a row of orange and two rows of green were added. I looked at it, turning it one way and then another, and I realized it did have the shape of a teapot, so I added the lip, another triangle and the handle, using orange and Outlining with green. The foot repeated the same colors. To add texture and interest I used green French Knots all around the oval-shaped pot, the handle to match the lighter shade of green French Knots used originally. Only two stitches were used, the Outline and French Knot, some places with more than one row to fill in the spaces.

The Gladiator design uses only three stitches, all three my favorites. For texture I used Outline Stitches of bright green and gold in single rows far enough apart so that the large Herringbone Stitches in brown showed through. The headgear has a halo of gold stars using the Cross Stitch, which is actually the Running Stitch going in different directions and crossing in the center. The light rust Running Stitches with plenty of off-white background fabric showing through were used for the face and neck. Bright green French Knots were used down the center front for texture and to add contrast of color.

The Mighty Oak design has plenty of texture, in fact in some places there are at least five thicknesses of yarn used in the trunk and branches of the tree, but each color shows through. The stitches were Chain and Detached Chain in three shades of gold and two of rust. The Outline Stitch was used in two lighter shades of gold on the tops of each branch to accent the area where the sun would be shining on it. The leaves were made with the Herringbone Stitch in rust lighter than the trunk and had gold Outline Stitches down the center of each leaf. (See color section.)

The Castle was inspired by the Camelot Inn in Tulsa, Oklahoma. Running Stitches, Herringbone, Bundle Stitch,

Chain, Outline and long and short Running Stitches contributed to the effect. The colors were shades of green, orange, rust and gold; favorite colors, but used in each stitchery for markedly different results. All were worked in a pattern form to give contrast; colors were more concentrated in window symbols. Most of the background was done in the Running Stitch, and because the background fabric was loosely woven it was easy to set a pattern and follow it. Background fabric showed through the windows where the Bundle Stitch was used, giving additional texture.

Daisies in the Field (shown in color) has just about everything in it. Color interest was achieved by using bright green knitting yarn with two shades of green crewel yarn to accent the shape of leaves and stems. The large white daisies were made with white knitting yarn with accents of blue, grayish white and yellow (all in long Running Stitches). The centers had large yellow French Knots with a darker shade of yellow and rust in tiny Running Stitches following the round shape in center. The outer edges were couched down with off-white crewel yarn using the Buttonhole Stitch, which gives a scalloped appearance. The butterflies were finally added to be in keeping with the delicate paintinglike feel of the stitchery—in Outline Stitches using yellow, turquoise, blue and gold metallic thread. Instead of leaving the gold showing completely, these outlines were couched down with a Running Stitch in blue. Thus the gold provides delicate highlights but is not overwhelming. The entire background was filled in with symbols of differently sized off-white Daisies in the Field far away from the five large ones showing in the complete stitchery. The background is filled in with the Single Feather Stitch, using three shades of green crewel and green sewing thread, as well as shades of yellow, beige and blue. In fact, all the colors of the daisies are repeated throughout the background.

Details of Harvest

Harvest (shown in color) was the first large stitchery that I attempted. I created interest by using a few shades of beige and shades of rust leading up to oranges to make the sky, where I interpreted the colors I had seen so often in western states. To paint with a needle, one must first observe. The entire sky was done in the Outline Stitch, letting bits of the background fabric show through. I made the stitch loose and in some places held the yarn above the needle, in other places, below. The colors were not placed in any particular pattern or design but I did shade them to accent certain areas. The sun behind the mountains was made with many, many rows of the Outline Stitch in shades of orange and light rust, and as I got close to the actual shape and color of the sun, I made the stitches closer together and in a darker shade. To cover the half shape of the sun close to the mountains, I used the square Chain Stitch.

As I worked on the mountain area, we were traveling extensively through Montana and its rolling hills were so impressive that I tried to interpret them by using the Herringbone Stitch exclusively, graduating in size. You really have to experiment with this type of building of stitch upon stitch; in some areas of Harvest many shades blend, letting earth tone colors come through. The desired feeling of depth, shadow and contour took two years to achieve. The entire background was made with vertical Running Stitches, about one inch long, using a pale shade of orange over it, to reflect the sun. Horizontally, in between rows of wheat, are three or more rows of yellow Outline Stitches. You can follow the use of each of the stitches we have learned by studying the full stitchery in the color section. A word about the trees is probably in order: I had never seen such trees but it is important to use and invent in creative stitchery. Creating something new is rearranging something old. How it is arranged depends upon your application of experience and your imagination.

COLLAGE AND APPLIQUE

What is collage? A combination of cut shapes arranged in a background. In creative stitchery, you put several related objects, shapes or cutouts on a piece of fabric and couch them. In making such a collage you may choose to express yourself freely, tell a story, make a composition out of mementos, or be frankly abstract in feeling and effect. Continue to arrange and rearrange until you feel satisfied with what you see: pin or glue in place and use any one of the Couching Stitches (Running, Outline, Feather, Herringbone, etc.).

Bits of flowers, shells, rocks, star fish, ceramics, glass, beads, ribbons, leaves and old lace lend themselves nicely. Motifs can be cut from lace without destroying the pattern; petals, leaves and so forth are quite charming. One day I plan to incorporate coins collected from travels, as symbols

MAKING THE STITCHERY

of various countries. Some students have used buttons as decorations and repeated designs in stitcheries; the design can be built around an unusual button's shape and color. Children have used leather for tree trunks, cork (which you can also sew *through*) in sea scenes, net and various found objects—the secret is simply the use of related materials. Some have used dried seeds and grasses, though many types of the latter are really too fragile.

A simple collage is the one we have seen on page 50. I found a piece of blue rickrack almost two inches wide and cut a piece of dark blue felt for background. To couch I used a small Running Stitch of a different shade blue. Looking at it from one direction, I saw an Indian motif, and rolling hills as in Montana, but the predominant suggestion was of water. Turning it in a horizontal position, since I was going to make water-related symbols across the bottom on one side of the tape, I made seven rows of long Running Stitches, spacing them evenly, for the bottom of the ocean going straight across the background. Above the rickrack, the Outline Stitch in the same color blue followed the wavy line of the tape, in three rows. Where the wave went down, I sewed three baby blue beads (to represent bubbles), one on top of the other, leaving a space between to balance the design. You have to let your imagination take over, but you can readily see what the symbols represent.

The possibilities in collage are many and again the word is don't be afraid to experiment—bright colors next to dull, three-dimensional shapes, trimmings such as fringe, chains or lovely crochet work just waiting in the linen closet; think of what you might do with that exquisite doily a grandmother once made with love and care. Making a collage is like building a house, starting with the foundation, and the only rules creating it that one need heed would be the rules of good design (balance in shapes and colors, harmony, etc.). Look to nature, consider how the Picassos and Braques achieve the effects in their work, dip into books on the principles of artistic composition, and try your own sense of arrangement.

Appliqué is applying a piece of fabric on top of another fabric and holding it in place with stitches. This method of design may have been discovered through necessity. A worn place in something valuable was covered with a patch. This is an excellent way to make use of scraps and small pieces of fabric and other materials, same as used in making a collage. To make it a part of the design and to add interest, texture, etc., different type stitches can be used, various thicknesses of thread can be applied. One sees progress when using

Angel in Flight. This is linear in feeling, rows of Outline making up the body of the design.

this method of designing, same as collage, using a combination of shapes.

Example: If the thread used matches the fabric you are applying, the shape will appear larger. If you want to soften the edge of the shape or shapes, small-size Buttonhole, Feather, Herringbone or Outline Stitch can be used. If you want to accent the shape and give it a more definite form, larger Couching or Outline Stitches in contrasting colors can be used. Sometimes more than one row will be needed. You can always add more rows if you like.

It is a good idea to start with one color and different shades and textures for contrast. If you feel that you are ready to mix and use a few contrasting colors, don't hesitate trying them. They can be cut and arranged on background fabric first and if you are not satisfied, keep moving and changing the cut pieces, letting some overlap in places. This is similar to putting together your own jigsaw puzzle. In fact, some pieces of fabric edges that do not ravel could be cut with pinking shears. After all, you will be working with scraps and if some do not work, they can be replaced so easily. A good source for such fabrics would be someone who does a lot of home sewing.

Any type fabric and materials can be used, including the background and decorative fabrics. If the edges of the fabric fray and ravel when cut, turn under, press and/or baste before stitching them to the background fabric. Again I want to remind you to plan on leaving enough margin for design to grow, not only with stitches but with added pieces of fabric. Some stitches can be extended from the shape for added interest. In making a leaf or flower design, the texture that each has, which can be seen in its natural form if viewed closely and which you may want to show with stitches on each leaf or petal, can be carried onto the background fabric.

PART THREE

Displaying a Stitchery

FINISHING A STITCHERY

SUPPLIES (also see complete list in back of book)

White vinegar	Scotchgard or substitute
Mild liquid soap	Teaspoon
Terry cloth towels	Tablespoon
Clean white cloth or old sheet	Iron
See-Thru-Steam-Thru press cloth	Ironing board
	Sponge
Rustproof straight pins (optional)	Plastic bag

WASHING

When your stitchery has been completed, remove the masking tape from the edges of the background fabric before washing it. Even though most colors of yarn are fade-proof, it is usually a good idea to take precautions and set the colors. You simply soak the finished stitchery in a basin full of cool water (enough to cover the stitchery completely), adding a few tablespoons of white vinegar. Let it soak for at least ten minutes.

It is now safe to pour a teaspoonful of mild soap into the vinegar water. Let the stitchery soak a few minutes longer before swishing it around and squeezing gently to remove the soil.

Then it is time to rinse *well*. If any soap happens to be left in the stitchery, it will discolor the fabric and yarn as you press it, turning it brown as if scorched. Make sure every bit of soap has been removed; the rinse water should be clear. Now squeeze out the surplus water and roll the stitchery in a terry cloth towel. You are ready for the next step, and it's best to proceed right away. If you do have to put your work aside, allow the stitchery to dry completely and then wet it down thoroughly, and place in a plastic bag to help even the moisture, when you find the time to proceed.

STEAM PRESSING

Cover your ironing board with a clean white cloth or sheet. If there are any stains on your ironing board cover, the steam will surely bring them out. This happened to me, and I found that you can remove a spot with a bit of Clorox—but do wash it out immediately, or it will disintegrate the fabric and yarn. Obviously, it's better to avoid this altogether.

Turn your iron to "cool" side of wool. I seldom use a hot iron even when I am working with linens. It may take a little longer, but you will be on the safe side. Do be cautious when you first start, for irons vary in heat controls. Synthetic background material will take less time and less heat than linen; if possible, test your iron's heat on a scrap of the material you have used.

It's a good idea to use the press cloth suggested on the list of supplies, for it affords added protection against scorching; an alternative would be a smooth thin white cloth. (The transparent and penetrating press cloth can be obtained from Leisure Products, Box 145, Ridgewood, New Jersey 07465.)

Place the stitchery, embroidery side up, on the clean white cloth, and secure it to the ironing board with rustproof pins. Be careful that you do not stretch the background fabric to a point where the design will lose its shape.

Start with the background fabric that is free of stitchery.

The dampness in the fabric will form steam when the warm iron touches the press cloth. (Have a clean sponge and some water close by, in case there are some dry areas or areas needing repressing.)

Press lightly, especially as you approach the stitchery area, for you do not want to flatten the stitches. A terry cloth towel is recommended to cushion the stitchery work while steam pressing.

When you have finished steam pressing the stitchery to your satisfaction, spread it out on a flat surface until totally dry.

SPRAYING

To protect the stitchery from getting soiled and to keep the colors bright, spray the stitchery. Since you have spent so many hours planning and making your piece, another step of protection is really worth it. Scotchgard or another type fabric spray can be used. Even if you plan to place the stitchery under glass, I would suggest spraying.

RECIPE FOR FIREPROOFING FABRIC: (can be used on completed stitchery, before steam pressing it)

9 ounces of borax   1 gallon water
4½ ounces boric acid

Dip fabric in solution and let drip dry. Repeat same process after each washing or dry cleaning.

I used this mixture in fireproofing some thin nylon curtain fabric which was used for steam pressing stitchery. It did not scorch or burn under a hot iron, but after using it a few times it did fall apart, which the See-Thru-Steam-Thru cloth does not do.

HEMS AND LININGS

HEMS

A hem can give any stitchery a finished look and helps maintain its shape. If a hem is deep enough and openings are left on both ends, a rod, strip of wood or some other device can be slipped through and used for hanging and support. In such a case, when a stitchery becomes a banner, you can sew your hem by hand or machine. A do-it-yourself book on making drapes would be an asset and an inexpensive way to see illustrated ways to hem and line a stitchery.

The cut edge of material must be even before measuring. Measure width of hem with a rule or card notched to indicate width desired. Allow one-half inch or more to be turned under if material is thin or is likely to fray.

Place pins where measurement was taken for width of hem.

Turn back and secure hem by pinning in place. The one-half inch allowed for turning under can be pressed or basted. Now sew a hem for each side of your stitchery.

If sides, top and bottom are to be hemmed, crease both hem edges and cut fabric away from corners to reduce the bulk when hem edges cross. Pin hem in place close to the edge where it will be sewn. The Back or Herringbone Stitch may be used to sew hem in place. When finished, remove pins.

If you do not have enough material for a hem, or if the piece is too heavy to be turned back, a false one can be made with a different type of material, ribbon or tape. This can be sewn by machine or by hand, using a Running Stitch at least one-half inch from the cut edge of the stitchery, putting right sides together. Make loose stitches, so material will not draw up and pull your stitchery out of shape. Turn back false hem and sew with a blind stitch.

If the background material of your stitchery is thin or flimsy, a lining will provide the needed body. Covering the back side of your work gives the stitchery a finished look, especially if there is not enough material for a proper hem.

Most background materials can also be used for lining.

Whatever you choose, if it is washable, do wash and press before cutting the size needed for lining, for it may shrink.

The stitchery should be completely finished and steam pressed *before* it is lined.

To allow the stitchery to fall smoothly, cut away or clip selvages of stitchery and lining. The lining at the bottom of the piece can be hemmed separately, or turned under and tacked. Cut lining the same size as stitchery, unless you need it longer for a separate hem in the bottom.

Lay stitchery on a clean flat surface, design side up.

Place lining top side down on top of stitchery, and pin the two pieces together, starting in the center and gradually working your way to outer edges. Pat with one hand while pinning with the other to keep both stitchery and lining flat. They must fit together or material will pull.

You can sew the pieces by hand or machine, going along sides and across top, leaving an opening at the bottom. If you place your pins crosswise along edges, material can be sewn on a machine without basting. Do not make stitches too small or tight—material would then pull. Make the seams at least one-half inch wide to keep them from pulling apart.

Dampen seams with a moist cloth or sponge and press.

Turn inside out, with top of stitchery facing you.

With your finger tips, flatten edges where seams were made, cover the seams with a clean cloth, dampen and press with a warm iron. All you have left to do is finish the bottom.

MOUNTING AND MATTING

I feel that the stitcheries I design and create with needle, yarn or thread are comparable to paintings. The only and proper place for an original painting would be on the wall, in an appropriate frame, and that is exactly how you can feel about your work. Each piece is an original and unique painting.

Having a collection of frames does help as you set about giving a stitchery the distinction it deserves. Then there are often smaller stitcheries which need a mat to set them off and make them large enough to fit the frames on hand or available ready-made. I often lay out an assortment of frames and place the different stitcheries in them to get an idea if shape and size will work. I try to visualize what the stitchery would look like neatly matted, perhaps in velvet. An experience years ago suggested the importance of quality in these finishing touches. I had won a few blue ribbons for my stitcheries in Montana and the state of Washington one year, and so the following year, I sent a few pieces again to the fair. When I received a red ribbon and the tag said, "What lovely and unusual work, but the frame is not suitable and does nothing for it," that made me think. I must do something that will enhance my work instead of detracting from it. That, too, is another reason why I say the framing of a stitchery must be a part of the total composition and be appealing to the eye.

SUPPLIES FOR MATTING AND MOUNTING

Matboard or substitute cardboard
Metal edge ruler

Mat cutter or substitute
Cutting board
Strip of matboard or piece of softwood board
Frame
Pencil
Newspapers
Rag
Cleansing tissue
Fine sandpaper

Extra supplies for covered mat: cotton-back velvet or other
    fabric and sharp, pointed scissors.

Matboard

You may of course purchase the standard 16- by 20-inch
size or larger matboard, in which case some cutting will be
necessary.

You may prefer a less expensive method of providing a matboard for your stitchery: Simply find yourself some cardboard boxes. This will require measuring, cutting, gluing together three, four or five pieces to achieve the right thickness of matboard. A spray adhesive or all-purpose glue can be used to glue one layer on top of the other. Allow to dry thoroughly.

If you plan to frame your stitchery, it is necessary that a piece of matboard be cut the same size as the completed stitchery to be used as a backing for it; attach the stitchery to a piece of matboard with a spray adhesive or Metylan wallpaper paste. If stitchery is larger than size frame you plan to use, for goodness' sake, don't cut it down. The edges can be turned back and glued to back of matboard.

Then if you decide you want the stitchery matted, a piece of matboard cut the same size as the one used in mounting the stitchery must be used. A covered mat will not only add size, but give a stitchery a more elegant and finished look. A contrasting color or one to match a color of yarn used will add interest to a completed stitchery. Although many type fabrics and materials are suitable for this purpose, cotton-back velvet was chosen to cover most of the mats used in this book, since velvet does enhance a stitchery made on linen. Felt was also used in covering the matboard for some stitcheries.

A third piece of matboard is cut the same size as the one used in mounting and/or matting the stitchery. This is the last thing placed in the frame for added support, before securing everything into place—the glass, if used, the mounted, matted or unmatted stitchery.

Note: In place of a third piece of matboard, a side of a corrugated paper box can be substituted.

THREE STEPS TO MOUNTING A STITCHERY

1 Measuring the Matboard: Measure the back inside space, the ledge of the frame, from side to side and from top to bottom, remembering the matboard must fit loosely *on* the ledge, but making sure that it will not slip through the frame. With a ruler, measure and pencil off the required size matboard.

2 Cutting Matboard: The cutting may sound easy, but it isn't. Matboard is fairly thick and cutting is slow going. First lay out some newspapers to protect the surface where you plan to work. On top, place a piece of plywood, masonite or formica; any one of these will make a good cutting surface.

Place a strip of matboard or softwood board under the matboard (area you plan to cut). This will cushion the blade as you cut through the matboard and help keep the point sharp, which is necessary in cutting matboard straight.

Place a metal edge ruler close to the penciled line. Hold the ruler and matboard firm to keep them from moving around while cutting.

Insert mat knife or substitute, keeping blade close to the edge of the ruler and pull the mat cutter, making one pass with the blade to ensure an even cut. If by chance, the blade does slip, a piece of fine sandpaper can be used to smooth the ragged edges.

3 Mounting a Stitchery: Now that you have the proper size piece of matboard (real or substitute), spray adhesive all over one side of the matboard. Be sure that you have a *fine coating* and that the larger droplets are sponged up with a piece of tissue, as these will soak through and discolor the

fabric. Be sure to read and follow the directions carefully on the can of spray adhesive, before using it.

Very carefully, with both hands, center the stitchery back side down on the adhesive-wet matboard, making sure it is straight. If you have to pull it up and put it back down again, you may need to spray on more adhesive. Let the freshly mounted stitchery dry completely before you frame it.

Note: When ready to glue the stitchery to the matboard, you can start at the top and work downward. Sometimes two people working together facilitate matters. One can hold the matboard in place as the other carefully lays the stitchery down on the adhesive-wet matboard.

Always experimenting, I recently discovered Metylan Wallpaper paste. Made by Standard Chemical Products, Inc., Hoboken, New Jersey 07030, this cellulose nonstaining wallpaper paste is very good to use in mounting a stitchery and matting with fabric. It is inexpensive and goes a long, long way. One important thing to remember: Follow directions on box for mixing and wait *at least fifteen minutes* before applying it with a brush, covering the entire area evenly.

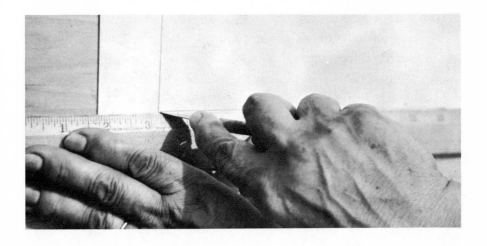

MEASURING AND CUTTING MATBOARD
FOR COVERED MAT

Remember, the matboard for a covered mat is cut the same size as the one cut for mounting the stitchery.

Measure the width of the border and where the opening or window would be.

Note: See "Cutting Matboard" above.

A piece of velvet was cut the same size as the matboard.

One side of the cut matboard was sprayed with all-purpose adhesive. The larger droplets were sponged up before the cut velvet was placed, back side down, on top of the adhesive-sprayed mat. Both hands were used in smoothing out the velvet, making sure there were no wrinkles. The nap of the velvet was brushed in one direction, before putting it aside to dry.

Then it was turned over to the back side and with a ruler one-half inch was measured and penciled off on the velvet from the edge of the opening. A razor blade was used to cut on the penciled lines. The piece of velvet cut from the center was then removed. On the one-half-inch-wide piece of velvet left showing on all four sides of the opening, a diagonal line was cut at all four corners. Then the velvet was pulled through to the back side and glued to the matboard, using some all-purpose adhesive (I do not suggest using spray adhesive here). A close check was made the entire time to make sure the velvet mat was smooth and taut on the right side and the corners were glued down to the back. Check carefully that the cut edges of velvet do not show on the right or top side of the mat. It takes a little pulling at the corners to have a neat velvet-covered mat.*

Suggestion: Use a clean rag while gluing velvet (on the back side) to matboard, to help keep fingers from sticking.

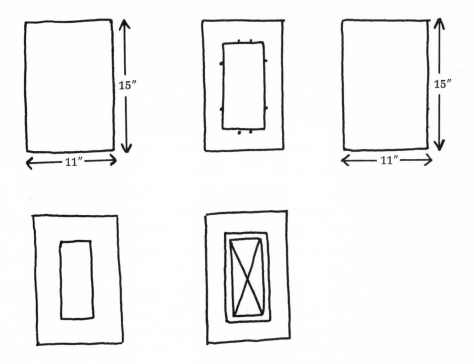

* Velvet has a tendency
to fray. To prevent this,
some glue can be used
(sparingly) along the edges
before placing the matted
stitchery in a frame.

INTRODUCTION TO FRAMING

My first challenge in framing accompanied an order for a motel—quite an undertaking for one with no experience. I had quite a few frames in the basement, but not enough to fill the order. The price I had given for the completed pictures, framed, was so ridiculously low. To save expense, I became a real scavenger. Someone was moving out of the city and I was lucky enough to come home with ten boxes filled with frames, some new and some old. Some were too small, but I put them all away and they really came in handy as I continued in creative stitchery. The scavenger became collector; I shopped every secondhand store, antique and thrift shop in the city and while traveling and purchased every frame for sale within a reasonable price. Then I had to figure out a way to repair those frames in poor condition. I applied methods I was using in fixing and antiquing old tables, chests and trays, and now the day has come when I may share experiences and hints picked up.

If you have done framing, you know the satisfaction that is derived from this task. You will also have learned, no doubt, that this saves a great deal of money besides giving you a second opportunity to display your artistic ability.

If you are limited to a choice of frames, it would be wise to place your stitchery (in the planning stages) in the frame you have to see that it will fit.

If you can afford it and need a special type and size frame, the best bet might be to have one custom-made. Less expensive and more fun, I find, is making your frame from scratch. Do look into the craft, using materials found or bought—from wood-turning shops, cabinet builders or lumber yards, where a wide range of moldings are available.

PAINTING A FRAME

1 Be sure to first check a frame to see if there are any rough places on it. If you should find some, they can easily be removed with a piece of medium-grade sandpaper. Make sure that you rub with the grain of the wood for a smoother finish. The wood dust can be removed with a rag dipped in some turpentine or mineral spirits, before you start with the finish for the frame.

2 You must remember that raw wood absorbs paint fast. To prevent this, apply one or two coats of wood sealer or shellac as a base coat (first coat) to seal the pores in the wood.

3 Paint the inside border first. Paint the outer edges next. Paint the top front side last.

Regardless of the type paint you are using, be sure to let each coat dry completely, before applying the next coat.

If you plan to use two or more coats of paint, for better adhesion, it is advisable to sand each coat lightly with fine- or medium-grade sandpaper (to remove the shine only, not the paint) before applying the next coat.

Any type paint can be painted over a lacquer finish, but lacquer will adhere only to a lacquer base, or it will act as a remover and make the paint underneath blister.

I learned this the hard way, but will never forget it as long as I live. There were two jars of gold paint, both jars the same size on a shelf. Not knowing that one was a lacquer-base paint and the other an oil base, I thought gold paint purchased in jars of this type were all alike. I really couldn't understand why sometimes the paint worked fine, then there were times it seemed to blister. The man at the paint store explained this to me. Now I am very cautious when purchasing paints. A hint to the wise is sufficient.

To remove a glossy finish, let paint dry for at least forty-eight hours, before rubbing it lightly with a piece of fine steel wool.

If you do not feel like removing the old finish from a frame that is in good condition, it can be sanded lightly, before applying a few coats of shellac or sealer to prevent the underneath color from bleeding through. Then frame is ready to be painted. Or use mixture of glazing compound and white undercoat with a bit of color added. It covers well over an old finish. Apply with dry brush method (very little paint on brush each time).

Aluminum paint can also be used to seal in the finish, before applying a new coat of paint.

To soften an old finish of paint, enamel or varnish, liquid sander can be used before applying a new finish. Be sure to follow directions on can carefully, before using it.

Although turpentine has been recommended to be used in mixing glazes for cleanup purposes including paintbrushes, which had been used in applying an oil-base paint, mineral spirits is less expensive and I have discovered that it will serve the same purpose with no problems involved.

When using metal-base enamels or paints, make sure that you keep a stick in the can and/or jar and stir it well each time you are ready to dip the brush in for more paint, because metal has a tendency to settle in the bottom.

If you plan to remove the old finish first, the quickest and best way to do it is to use a paint and varnish remover that removes any finish. Make sure you read the directions on the can *carefully* before using it.

Wonders will never cease. In the past two years most of the paint manufacturers ceased making color in oil for tinting paints. The only source is in an art supply store. The product they use now is really more functional. It is called universal colorant, which comes in all colors and can be mixed with anything, water, turpentine, etc. I do think it is an improvement. If you keep color in oil tubes around for any length of time the linseed oil starts seeping through and you really have a sticky mess. So a salute to the chemists who are constantly making new and better discoveries for us to enjoy. For mixing colors, my preference is Color in Oils.

Masking tape can be used on a frame, if you feel that the brush full of paint will spread into an area that you do not wish to cover with that particular color. Have you ever seen professional painters use it on windows? The same can be put on the glass of a frame to keep paint from smudging it.

Have you ever thought of making a drying rack for your frames? You may want to make one, since it is useful for many things. It would keep a freshly painted frame (sides) from sticking to newspaper, if too much paint was used and it would drip down the sides. (Great for painting trays, too.)

Any type of board will do. Use some long thin finishing nails. Hammer them through the board, and the frame can rest on the points of the nails, which will be sticking out. You must be careful in putting them away, so no one will accidentally sit on a board; that really could result in a tragedy. I keep them in pairs and place one on top of the other for storage.

Light gray and pastel colors can all be made the same way. Begin with white, using the amount of paint you think will be needed. (A word to the wise is sufficient, so on the safe side, it is better to have some left over.)

Pour the amount you plan on using into a clean can. (I keep several of the same size cans stacked in a cabinet and when one is needed, I don't have to start looking.)

Start by adding *drop* by *drop* (use black in making gray), stirring well each time you add a drop. You want to remember that the color or colors you are using are concentrated. When you think the right shade has been mixed, stop. You must remember one thing, that *paint dries darker*. Sometimes in trying to match something perfectly, I will paint a board first and let it dry to make sure it is the right shade.

A very good thing to remember is that grayed colors are softer. A painter once told me that and I haven't forgotten it. So if you want a soft shade, add some black to the paint, but *be careful* not to put in too much at a time or you will defeat your purpose. It takes time and patience but it is worth the effort you put into your work.

If you are using an oil-base paint, the brush can be cleaned with mineral spirits or turpentine. It is then advisable to wash the brush in warm soapy water and rinse well before putting it away. Then you are sure to have a workable brush, one that is not stiff.

There is a brush cleaner that may alleviate the problem, if you forgot to clean the brush you used before putting it away. Follow the directions on the box, and if the brush is not in a bad condition, you may salvage it. It is always worth a try. I have had good luck at times, but I must admit not every time.

A brush that has been used with a latex, casein-type or water-base paint can be cleaned in warm soapy water and rinsed thoroughly, after using it.

If you have used a lacquer, the brush must be cleaned in lacquer thinner *only*, then follow the same procedure used for other brushes, washing and rinsing in water before putting it away.

If shellac has been used, clean brush in denatured alcohol and again follow the same procedure that is used for all paintbrushes, regardless of size or type brush used.

PAINTED FRAME (FOR FREE FORM DESIGN)

Unfinished frame 1 by 12 by 20 inches
Small tube burnt umber color in oil or universal colorant
Small can turpentine
Small can satin-finish varnish
Small can wood sealer
Teaspoon
Medium-grade sandpaper
Paintbrushes
Empty cans
Rags
Newspapers

1 Frame was sanded to remove a few rough spots. Wood dust was wiped away with rag dipped in turpentine.

Wood sealer was applied with a brush and put aside to dry overnight.

2 A teaspoon of burnt umber was mixed with three teaspoons turpentine and one teaspoon varnish in a clean empty can. This mixture was put on the frame with a brush, making sure the entire frame was covered. The warm brown (burnt umber) color matched the background fabric used for this design. This was painted twice.

3 Two coats of satin-finish varnish were applied as a finish, letting first coat dry completely before applying another coat.

NATURAL WOOD FINISH FRAME

Unfinished frame 1¼ by 6 by 7 inches
Can of boiled inedible linseed oil
Clean pan or can
Hot plate or stove
Medium sandpaper
Newspapers
Rags

1 See "Painting a Frame," but be sure *not* to use wood sealer.

2 Pour a small amount of linseed oil in a clean pan. Place it over a low flame to keep oil hot the entire time you are using it.

Dip a rag in the hot oil and *rub* briskly into the already sanded frame making sure you *fill in* all grooves (raw wood pores).

Repeat the same process three or more times, depending on how much it takes for the frame to feel smooth to the touch of the hand. Set the frame away from heat to dry overnight, after *each* application of oil.

(*Note:* Cornstarch can be mixed in with the hot oil, to act as a filler.)

Caution: Oil-soaked rags are subject to spontaneous combustion, so do be careful. To avoid a possible fire hazard, it is important that you promptly discard them in a water-filled container or burn them.

3 Polish with a soft cloth until frame shines.

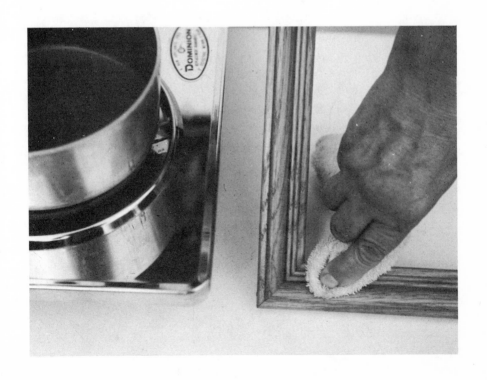

GOLD FINISH FRAMES

Frame   Turpentine
Gold metal enamel or gold   or mineral spirits
    liquid leaf (both come   Paintbrush
    in different shades   Satin-finish varnish
    of gold)   Empty can
Newspapers   Rags
Stick for stirring enamel   Soap and water (optional)

Whenever I am in doubt as to the color that would be best suited for a stitchery frame, I use gold. It will complement any color used in a design. It does not matter what the original finish is, because both the gold metal enamel and the liquid leaf will cover any clean surface. To protect the finish from oxidizing, which will happen after a period of time, a few coats of satin-finish varnish can be applied. I have had good results using the gold enamel and it is much cheaper than the gold liquid leaf.

1 If you are using an old frame, make sure you wash it first, then check it for repairs. See p. 160.

Note: If you use a new frame, see p. 145.

2 Apply at least two coats of gold metal enamel or liquid gold leaf paint, letting each coat dry thoroughly before applying another. This is also a good time to do some experiments with texture for different effects, if you so desire.

(*Note:* See information on p. 159.)

3 This is the last thing you do to the frame: Apply at least two coats of satin-finish varnish. Then you will have a frame that is functional and can be used anywhere and with all colors.

OLD FRAME WITH METALLIC FINISH
(FOR IVY VINE DESIGN)

Old frame 1 by 10½ by 21 inches
Soap and water
Turpentine or mineral spirits
Gold metal enamel
Silver metal enamel
Satin-finish varnish
Medium-grade sandpaper
Rags
Empty can
Liquid sander
Newspapers
Paintbrushes
Stick for stirring

An old frame was selected to be used for the Ivy design, because of its shape and size. It was in good condition, therefore needed no repairs. See p. 145.

1 After frame was washed and dried, liquid sander was applied with a brush to soften the old finish. Make sure you read and follow directions on can carefully before using, even though you may be familiar with the product.

Equal amounts of gold and silver metal enamel were mixed together in a clean empty can. The mixture was stirred well each time before dipping the brush in for another load, as metal does have the tendency to settle in the bottom.

Even though in this case I did use equal amounts of each color, the proportion can vary. You be the judge of how you want your frame to look. There are no set rules to follow. The only important thing that you must remember is to *use products that mix*. (Don't forget my experience with the two jars of metal enamel.)

2 Two coats of the gold and silver metal enamel were applied to the frame. For the smooth finish, each coat of enamel was put on with brush strokes going in one direction only.

3 Two coats of satin-finish varnish were put on to protect the finish.

ANTIQUING

This is a wonderful way to get texture with so little expenditure of time and money. Regardless of the original condition of the frame, with this process you can have something that looks beautiful and custom-made.

For the base (at least two undercoats), a flat, vinyl or casein-type paint can be used. It should be in a light color, so when you use the glaze on top, the color will show through. I have often used off white, but once I used the same vinyl burnished gold as the undercoat (yellow with a small amount of black mixed with it) which was the color used on the newly decorated walls of my home. This served perfectly with an avocado green mixture glaze. To give it highlights, I used a weak mixture of gold bronze powder, turpentine and a small amount of varnish. To seal in the glaze and as the finish, I applied two coats of satin-finish varnish. (See p. 145.)

Antique glazes can be made by mixing, on the average, one part of color to two parts of turpentine or mineral spirits and less than one-half the amount of satin-finish varnish as of the color used. A *little* more or less of each would have no effect on the glaze. Consistency will depend on how thick or dark a glaze you will want. Experiment. Once you decide on the color and consistency, be sure to mix enough at one time, so when you do start to do the glazing, you will not run out of the mixture. One important thing: *Do not use too much varnish* in mixture. The glaze mixture should be "watery" (not sticky) so when applied with a brush only, it can be brushed back and forth until you are satisfied with the results and have acquired that antique look. Keep a rag close at hand so excess glaze can be wiped from the brush. You need a dry brush to get the right texture.

DISPLAYING A STITCHERY

ANTIQUE FRAME (FOR CATTAILS DESIGN)

Unfinished frame, 1 by 11 by 14 inches
Raw sienna universal colorant
Medium-grade sandpaper
Off-white flat paint
Turpentine or mineral spirits
Satin-finish varnish

Paintbrushes
Rags
Wood sealer
Empty can
Newspapers
Spoon

1 See "Painting a Frame" and "Antiquing."

2 Two coats of off-white paint were applied to frame.

3 An antique glaze was made with raw sienna. It was applied to frame with a brush. After a few minutes, the glaze was wiped off with the *brush*, leaving streaks of raw sienna in places.

4 Two coats of satin-finish varnish were applied over the glaze to seal in the color and as a finish. Again I want to remind you that any color or mixture of colors can be used the same way.

Hint: If you plan on antiquing a frame and do not want to remove the finish, it is possible to do so by using the following formula:

½ pint glazing compound
2 tablespoonsful white undercoat paint
Bit of color

Use liquid sander or sandpaper frame to remove the shine for better adhesion. Apply the glazing compound mixture. Let dry.

ANTIQUE GRAY TEXTURE

Frame (unfinished)
White casein-type or flat
   paint
Gray casein-type or flat
   paint
Newspapers
Spoon

Black colorant for making
   gray paint
Medium-grade sandpaper
Large-size screw
Rags
Can
Paintbrush

1 Scratch frame for texture, using the side of a screw. Make the grooves as deep as you want them to be. You be the judge. It is advisable to scratch with the grain in the wood.

2 Sand away only the splinters and small rough spots, being careful not to remove the grooves that you just made, to get the texture you are aiming for.

3 Paint the entire frame with one coat of white paint, making sure the grooves are well filled. Before the paint dries, wipe *only* the *surface* of the frame with a rag, being careful not to remove any paint from the grooves.

4 When first coat of paint is dry, sand lightly for better adhesion, before applying one coat of gray paint. See "Painting a Frame."

Let stand for ten minutes, before wiping off the gray paint with a clean rag. Polish frame with a soft rag.

It is easy to do and does not require much of your time in finishing a frame with this type finish.

Note: Try using other colors following the same procedure. For added interest, wormwood texture could be used; this is only a suggestion.

WORMWOOD EFFECT

Black universal colorant
   (mixes with anything)
   or substitute color in oil
Flat container
Old comb or knife
Spoon

Turpentine or substitute
Old toothbrush
Can
Newspapers
Rags
Satin-finish varnish

1 Lay out plenty of newspapers. Make a watery mixture using black colorant and turpentine or substitute, and pour into a flat container. (One part color to three or four parts turpentine.)

2 Dip a toothbrush into the watery mixture. Take a comb or knife and rub it across the toothbrush. It is advisable to try it on newspapers, before putting it on the frame. Then you can decide what size specks (wormholes) they should be. That would be your decision. If you are not satisfied, wipe it off while still wet and start over again.

3 Apply a few coats of satin-finish varnish to seal in the specks of paint applied for wormwood effect.

Note: Other colors can be used. More than one color can be used for a speckled effect. Make sure one color has dried before another is applied.

TARNISHED METALLIC FINISH

Frame
Wood sealer or shellac
White, gray and red flat paint
Blue, ocher, black and burnt
   umber color in oil or
Universal colorant (mixes with
   anything)
Turpentine or mineral spirits
Silver (aluminum bronze powder)

Paintbrushes
Newspapers
Cans
Spoon
Rags
Satin-finish varnish

1 See "Painting a Frame." Apply one coat wood sealer or shellac.

2 Apply one coat of white paint to frame. Let dry.

3 Apply one coat of light gray paint and let dry.

4 Apply a *heavy* coat of red paint and let dry.

5 Apply streaks of blue, ocher, black and silver paint, making sure each color is dry, before applying another. (One ounce aluminum bronze powder to two ounces turpentine and one teaspoon varnish.)

6 For that tarnished silver look, apply equal parts burnt umber colorant or color in oil and turpentine to the frame with a rag. If you put on too much, it can be wiped off. This is a good time to do some experimenting.

7 Apply two coats of satin-finish varnish.

Now aren't you happy that you did take the time necessary in finishing a frame like this? Remember that other colors can be used in place of the ones given on the supply list.

REPAIRING OLD FRAMES

You may have an old picture frame which could be used. It is not necessary to spend a fortune in getting an old frame in good condition. It does require time and patience, but again, from experience, it certainly is worth it. Be sure to follow the instructions on how you, too, can salvage, repair and refinish a frame to your satisfaction.

1 Remove old wire, glass, if there is any, screw eyes and brads before washing the frame in a solution of soapy water; rinse well and put aside to dry away from the heat, before you start to make repairs.

2 Now you are ready to check the frame for sturdiness (connecting corners). If it seems to be a bit wobbly, it would be advisable to put in a few extra brads for better support. Before nailing in the brads, I like to use some wood glue first. I use my finger to force it in between the connecting corners, even if it means pulling frame apart a bit.

Be careful in doing this, because you do not want the brads to come through the frame. The size brad to use will depend upon the thickness of the frame. I have found that miter braces are useful, one for each corner of frame, to keep it straight until glue is dry.

3 If you remove the old finish, see "Painting a Frame."

4 Fill in all nail holes and damaged places with wood putty or substitute. Read and follow directions on the can.

Suggestion: If the frame you are using has nicks, scratches and even parts that are missing and you want something different and original, instead of filling in damaged areas, add more distressed areas to correspond with the existing ones.

WAYS TO CREATE TEXTURE

STREAKING, STIPPLED AND MARBLEIZED EFFECT

Texture can be created by dabbing and twisting a brush, sponge, rag or scrap of carpet with paint or glaze. One or more colors can be used, but make sure that some of each color you use shows. In refinishing some old frames, I have used gold and silver metal enamel paint with a touch of brown. Or you can use gold by itself, keep working the paint, even when it gets tacky. You can go over a dried coat of gold to further deepen texture. After the last coat is completely dry, two coats of varnish can be applied to keep the gold from oxidizing.

CROSSHATCH

I have used this method a number of times. Over a light base color, I have used gold antique glaze and applied it sparingly with a brush, first going in one direction only (from side to side), and while the glaze was still wet, with the brush, I then went in the opposite or cross direction, from top to bottom. For the final coat, as usual, one or more coats of satin-finish varnish.

SPATTER PAINTING (similar to Wormwood Effect)

Use an old toothbrush to apply the same thin mixture that would be used for wormwood effect. Rub the brush back and forth over a wire screen. It would be advisable to practice on newspapers. More than one color can be used, letting each color dry before another is applied.

Antiquing Kit

This is an alternative but more expensive method.

Applied Texture

These suggestions have been used with success on frames, furniture, etc. Old jewelry such as earrings can be used, after the backs are removed. Use them in the four corners where the frame is joined. They can be left in their natural state and also painted to match the frame or to contrast with it (as in gold, copper or silver). Epoxy glue can be used to secure them to the frame.

Decorative Nails

These nails with rounded heads come in colors and also in brass. They come in various sizes; a pattern can be made using them. Be careful while nailing them in place. Place the sharp end of the nail where you wish it, cover with a thick cloth and hammer through the thickness to keep from marring frame or nail.

Try all sorts of hardware, including water hose rubber washers (cut them in half and glue them to the background with epoxy glue, then paint as part of the background), plastic curtain rings (I have used different sizes and painted them the same color as frame). Very effective and so inexpensive.

SHADOW BOX OF OLD FRAMES
(FOR CITY ABSTRACT DESIGN)

Two old frames:
  one 2½ by 19½
  by 23½ inches
  one 1 by 16 by 20 inches
Tube of manganese blue
  and earth green color
  in oil or universal
  colorant (mixed the
  two colors together to
  obtain color to match
  the turquoise yarn
  used in stitchery)
Small can off-white
  dull-finish paint

Can liquid sander
Turpentine or mineral
  spirits
Satin-finish varnish
Soap and water
Gold metal enamel paint
Paintbrushes
Newspapers
Hammer
Nails
Empty cans
Rags
Stick

1 After the two frames were cleaned and repaired, they were nailed together, one inside of the other. The purpose was to make a shadow-box-type frame for City Abstract design. The nails had to be hammered in on a slant, to keep them from coming through the frames (front side).

Note: See information on "Repairing Old Frames."

2 Liquid sander was used to soften the old finish. Take time to read the instructions on the can before using it. For best results follow directions carefully.

3 See information under "Painting a Frame."

Apply one coat of off-white paint with a brush and set the frame aside to dry. See "Antiquing."

The next day a mixture of antique glaze was made to match the color (turquoise) yarn that was used in the stitchery and to blend with the raw-silk covered mat.

4 The mixture of antique glaze was applied to the frames with a brush, making different type strokes, working back and forth until I was satisfied with the end results. Then the frames were set aside to dry.

5 Two coats of satin-finish varnish were applied to seal in the color and to protect the finish.

6 The inner edge of the frame was painted with gold metal enamel to complement the turquoise in the stitchery and the finish of the frame.

FRAMES DECORATED WITH PLASTER DESIGNS

You may have a frame that has raised plaster designs on it, but a few are missing, and you would like to know how to replace them. If you follow the directions carefully and have the time and patience needed to repair the frame, here is your chance.

1 Grease a section of the design, which is similar to the one you want replaced, with vaseline or substitute, so clay impression can be removed easily.

2 Place some regular or plastic modeling clay over the greased section. To make a good impression, press the clay down well with your finger tips.

3 Mix plaster of Paris with some water to make a creamy solution. (It is advisable to mix it in a container that can be thrown away. If poured down the drain, the plaster may clog it.) Put the mixture into the clay mold with a spoon, making sure no air bubbles form. Let dry several hours, before removing molded design from the clay. *Be careful* that you do not break or chip the plaster mold, because it does become brittle when dry and will chip easily. The edges of the newly cast design can be sanded if you should have a problem fitting it into the space.

4 Remove the design carefully because glue will have to be applied to frame to hold it (design) in place. If there are any rough spots, let dry thoroughly before sanding them away carefully with a piece of fine-grade sandpaper.

5 Paint the new part with two coats of sealer or shellac to keep paint from soaking into plaster. Frame is then ready to be finished.

See information on "Painting a Frame."

Alternate Method

If the plaster-decorated frame is in really bad shape and it is impossible to get a matching impression for a mold, it can still be used. Chip away the remaining designs down to the bare wood. Sand away the splinters (with the grain) and you will have a lovely textured frame that can be finished to your liking.

See information on "Painting a Frame."

FRAMING WITH GLASS

There are a number of reasons why some of my stitcheries are framed under glass. After completing my first Ivy Vine design and weaving in the background (the holes in the fabric were large) with off-white needlepoint yarn, I wanted to protect it. At the time I did not know about Scotchgard. The stitchery is framed with a nonglare Trusite glass, so that reflections from a lamp close by will not detract.

Another reason for framing under glass is: It will help preserve and protect the work of art, if framed properly and if it is airtight, because some types of heat (gas especially) have a tendency to cause colors to fade and sometimes change them completely.

If you want children and even grownups to keep hands off, what better way is there to protect your work? People have a tendency to touch things, especially if they are of an unusual quality and texture. Glass is easy to care for.

You do not have to spend a lot of money to frame a stitchery using glass as a protection. I have used glass from old frames, sometimes cutting the glass down to correct size. If a piece of glass is broken and there is still enough left, I never throw it away, because at some future date, I will be needing glass for a frame.

Note: I keep my smaller pieces of glass in old metal record stands, "filed" according to size. The larger pieces I keep in the same type box that window glass is packed in. I get them from a glass distributor (free).

If necessary, you can have glass cut to the size you need. Sometimes I get many nice size pieces of glass that glass distributors are throwing away and I am able to use. So, you see, if you know where and how to shop, it can be economical.

Tru-site glass (nonglare) or
    window glass (single
    or double strength)
Carpet (surface for cutting)
Glass cutter
Ammonia, vinegar or
    glass wax

Metal edge ruler
Rags
Newspapers
Lubricating oil
Marking (grease) or
    eyebrow pencil

Steps in Cutting Glass

1 Place glass on padded surface (carpet). Dip cutter in oil (cuts better). Size can be measured and marked with a grease or eyebrow pencil, or use a metal edge ruler where you want to cut. *With pressure* make *one line* with glass cutter. Turn glass over on opposite side and tap *lightly* in center of line made. Holding the glass with hand on either side, gently exert pressure on the cracked line and the glass will separate. This is not easy to do. The important thing to remember is to make *one straight line* with your glass cutter to get an even cut. Size glass must fit on ledge (shelf) in back of frame.

2 Wash glass with water mixed with ammonia, vinegar or glass wax to remove the grease, lint and finger marks. Then polish both sides with a clean lintless rag or newspapers. *Suggestion*: Place one edge of glass next to you (at the waist) and hold it there with one hand and use the other hand for polishing the glass. This gives you the opportunity to see that the glass is spotless.

3 Place the glass in frame, being careful not to get finger marks on it, or it will have to be cleaned again.

4 Place the stitchery with embroidery side down touching the glass. Then you are ready to finish your framing.

STEPS IN FRAMING A STITCHERY

Stitchery must be *mounted* if it is to be framed. It does not have to be matted.

Frame with or without glass

Stitchery: mounted and matted

Screw eyes

Picture wire

Scotchgard spray or substitute

Brads

Hammer

Masking tape

Wire cutter

OPTIONAL SUPPLIES

Bulldog picture hangers

Diamond glazier points (come in different sizes)

Brown wrapping paper or grocery bag

Point setter

Cardboard or corrugated paper

1 Spray completed stitchery a few times on both sides to protect it against soil regardless of whether it will be placed under glass for protection or framed without glass. First be sure to read all directions on the can of spray.

2 The stitchery is placed in the frame (if framing with glass, do that first).

3 To hold everything together in the frame, you will need some brads and a hammer. The length of the brads will depend on the thickness of the frame. These brads must be nailed into the inside edge of the frame. Drive them in only halfway into this side edge; the other half sticking out is what holds everything together. Space them two to four inches apart on each side.

If you happen to know someone who has a point setter, it can be used instead of brads—this is a far easier method.

4 Use strips of masking tape over brads or diamond points to hold them in place and to make a neat finish.

BACKING FOR FRAME (OPTIONAL)

A piece of cardboard or corrugated paper can be cut the same size as the matboard used in mounting the stitchery and used as a backing before putting in brads. Then continue, following the steps as above.

After stitchery has been secured in the frame, a piece of brown wrapping paper can be cut a bit smaller than outer edge of frame and glued to the back of the frame and not to the cardboard. Be sure to remove any old paper on the back of the frame before gluing down new paper, or glue will act as a remover and pull up the old paper left (glued to frame). This gives the whole job a really professional look and helps keep glass-framed work clean. It would be advisable to do this before wiring.

Before the finished stitchery can be hung up for display, the back will need to be wired. If you need help, why not use another wired frame as a model?

Steps in Wiring a Frame

1 Two screw eyes are needed and some picture wire. Measure the width of the frame and add at least four inches to the length of the wire before cutting it. For a small frame, measure about three inches down from top of frame on both sides, where the screw eyes will go. The places can be marked with a pencil or sharp end of nail. The length of screw eyes will depend on the thickness of the frame. Remember, you do not want them to be too long, or they will come through and ruin your frame.

2 Insert the screw eyes and turn them slowly (they will break off if you are not careful) until only the eyes are showing. Pull the picture wire through the screw eyes, allowing a few inches on each side for wrapping wire around itself to hold it in place.

Bulldog picture hangers can be used in place of the screw eyes and picture wire. Make sure that you measure exactly with a ruler the center of the frame (at top). Then it is a good idea to place the hanger down on frame, centering it (it is marked on hanger) and make a pencil mark in each hole where it will be nailed to the frame. This is a faster, easier method in getting a frame ready for hanging.

MOUNTING AND DISPLAYING A STITCHERY

There are other ways of displaying stitcheries. If the background fabric and the yarns that you used are of the heavy type and you plan to hang your work in an informal setting such as a family room, you probably would like to hang it in a more rustic manner, to fit the decor.

MOUNTING ON BOARD

You can mount your stitchery on a piece of chipboard, masonite or plywood (making sure the plywood has been seasoned so it will not warp). Cut the board at least one-half inch smaller (depending on thickness of board) than the stitchery so edges can be pulled to back side of board and glued down for a neater finish. Apply glue with a brush or applicator to the back side of the board. Use a clean sponge or cloth if necessary to keep stitchery clean while gluing it to the board. Stitchery can then be framed or hangers applied before displaying it.

HANG STITCHERY USING DRIFTWOOD

Driftwood should be soaked, washed and *dried* before using a wood sealer to close the pores of the wood. Branches from a tree can be used for the same purpose. Stitchery can be stapled, tacked or loops of yarn or fabric can be used to hold stitchery in place. Displaying a stitchery this way can be very unusual and different. Sometimes planning stitchery to fit the driftwood works out satisfactorily. Back of driftwood can be wired for hanging.

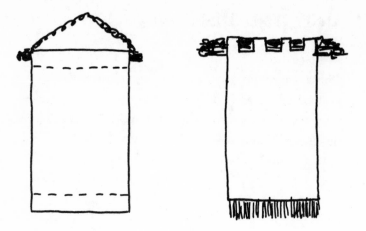

Dowel rods, curtain rods and window shade slats can be used at the top and bottom of a stitchery. It can be held in place with loops as hangers or a hem made and the rod slipped through it. On each end where rods extend, if made of wood, a small groove can be made to keep rope or cord from slipping off.

A fancy cord or rope can be made by twisting or plaiting yarn. The ends can be tied and fringed or tied and stitched to keep them from pulling apart.

Loops can be made from background fabric and fastened onto rod with buttons, snaps or even sewed in place.

End decorations can be attached with glue or thin brads. Wooden beads, old jewelry and papier-mâché ornaments can be used.

HANG LIKE A BANNER

Felt or other type materials that do not fray or ravel when cut are functional in using stitchery to be hung as a banner. A sword, horn, fancy curtain rod, dowel rod

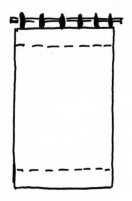 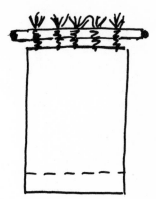

(pole) or window shade slats with end decorations can be used as a hanger.

1 Make a deep hem at top, so a hanger will slide through with ease. A hem can be put in by hand or machine.

2 Measure and mark off even spaces on the hem. If hem happens to be three inches deep and stitchery is nineteen inches wide, spaces two inches apart can be made.

3 Cut away every other block, making sure you leave one on each end for support. *Be careful* not to cut into the stitches of the hem.

4 You may have already planned the design for this stitchery. Yes or no? Now is the time to get it centered, so completed stitchery will hang properly.

5 The bottom of the stitchery can be finished off with a plain hem, cut into shapes, or fringe can be added. If you should decide to use fringe, I would suggest matching a color of yarn used in the stitchery or choosing a complementary one.

Appendix

BASIC STITCHERY SUPPLIES

Supplies	Uses	Where to buy
BEESWAX OR CANDLE: Optional	To stiffen fluffy yarn for easy threading	
CARBON: Dressmaker's sheet of red, blue, yellow and white in each package *or* carbon paper	To transfer design from tracing paper to background fabric	Notions
CHALK: White and colors	To draw design on background fabric	Stationery
CLIPS: Paper	To hold papers together while tracing design (keep from slipping)	Stationery
CRAYONS: Washable and nontoxic	Drawing designs	Stationery
COMPASS: Optional	Making geometric designs	Stationery
DYES: Commercial or homemade	For dyeing yarns	Drug
FABRICS: Background, list on page 62	Stitcheries	Drapery or yard goods
FIXATIVE: Clear matte spray fixative or hair spray	To keep pencil and chalk designs from smudging	Art supply
HOOP: Optional	To keep background fabric from drawing up while stitching	Needlework
MAGNIFYING GLASS	To look at designs in nature more closely	Camera
MICROSCOPE: Optional	To look at designs too small to be seen with the naked eye	Toy

PAPER:	Drawing designs	Art supply or
Drawing, typewriter, plain wrapping, etc.	Cut paper patterns Increasing or decreasing a design	stationery
Graph	Increasing or decreasing a design, sketch or patterns	Stationery
Scratch pads; 4- by 6-inch size recommended	Sketches	Stationery
Plain colored papers	Cut paper pattern designs	Art supply
Tracing pad (transparent, parchment type) by the yard *or* width *or* onionskin *or* thin typing paper	To place over design for tracing	Art suppy or stationery
PEN: Ball point, color of ink different than one used in design (contrast)	To trace design (on paper) onto background fabric	Stationery
PENCILS: No. 2 (soft lead)	For sketching and drawing designs	Stationery
Col-Erase (assorted colors)	Draw designs on background fabric or paper	Art supply
Carbon (assorted colors)	To make your own carbon designs	
PINS: Straight rustproof and/or safety	To hold cut paper patterns to background fabric	Notions
	To hold yarn design on background fabric	

PLASTIC BAGS: Clear	To store yarns, threads and stitchery	
SCISSORS:		
Long pointed, 6 inches (average size)	To cut paper, patterns and fabric	Notions
Short pointed, 3 inches (average size)	To cut yarn and thread	
TAPE: Masking, at least ¾ inch wide *or* Magic transparent	To keep cut edges of fabric from raveling To hold fabric, carbon and tracing paper in place while transferring design	Stationery
THIMBLE: Optional	To protect finger from needle while sewing	Notions
TRIANGLE: Clear plastic, comes in 2 sizes	To draw geometric designs	Art supply
YARN		Yarn

SUPPLIES FOR FINISHING AND FRAMING A STITCHERY

Supplies	Uses	Where to Buy
ADHESIVES:		
Multipurpose spray (white or clear)	To mount stitchery on matboard, plywood, chipboard, masonite	Stationery
Metylan Cellulose Wallpaper paste (clear, nonstaining)	To glue cardboard together as substitute matboard	Wallpaper
All-purpose white or clear glue	To glue covering on back of matboard To glue brown kraft paper on back of frame To glue cardboard together as substitute matboard	Stationery
EPOXY	To glue decorations on frames and dowel rods	Stationery
AMMONIA: Household 15 per cent ammonia, vinegar. or glass wax	To clean frames To clean glass for frame	Grocery
BRADS: Thin wire nails without heads; come in different sizes	To hold mounted and/or matted stitchery in frame To hold corners of frame together when repairs are made	Hardware
BRUSHES: Natural bristle; come in assorted sizes; ½ to 2 inches, depending on size of frame	For painting frame For applying glazes For applying glue For texture painting For varnishing For shellacking	Paint

BRUSHES:

Artist's camel or red sable No. 1 (round); comes in larger sizes	Painting lines and narrow areas (spaces)	Art supply
Stencil No. 2 (optional)	For texture painting	Art supply
Old toothbrush	For spatter painting (wormwood effect) To clean grooves in frames For texture painting	
Old stiff varnish (cut away some bristles and leave ragged edges)	For streaking paint (texture)	
CANS: Clean, empty	For mixing glazes For mixing paints For cleanup purposes (brushes, etc.) To warm linseed oil in To mix plaster of Paris For mixing wood putty	
CARPET SCRAPS	For texture painting Can be substituted for a brush To cushion surface while cutting glass	Rug
CLAMPS: Miter corner	To hold and keep corners of frame squared (even) while repairing frame	Hardware
CLAY: Regular or plastic modeling	To make a mold in repairing a frame	Art supply
COMB: Old	For texture painting in applying wormwood effect	

CUTTING BOARD: Plywood *or* other softwood *or* matboard	Makes a good surface for cutting mats (cushions blade of mat cutter)	Lumber
CUTTING TOOLS:		
Glass cutter	To cut glass	Hardware
Mat cutter (Dexter *or* Stanley mat knife) *or* single-edge razor blade or X-acto Knife	To cut matboard To cut cardboard To cut corrugated board	
Scissors, sharp point	To cut fabrics To cut yarn To cut paper	Notions
Wire *or* pliers with wire cutter	To cut picture wire	Hardware
DECORATIVE ITEMS: Beads (wooden, glass, ceramic), plastic curtain rings, nails, hose washers	To use as end decorations for dowel rods to hang stitchery For raised and textured effect on frames	Junk, Jewelry, Hobby shops
DETERGENT: Heavy duty Mild	To remove grease and dirt from old frames To wash stitchery	Grocery
FABRICS: Cotton-back velvet, felt, burlap and other types	To cover matboard for added interest and color	Yard goods or drapery
FRAMES: Standard sizes can be purchased, some with precut mats	To frame a stitchery for hanging	Frame
5 by 7 inches 7 by 9 inches 8½ by 11 inches 11 by 14 inches 16 by 20 inches	6 by 8 inches 8 by 10 inches 10 by 12 inches 12 by 12 inches 18 by 24 inches	
GLASS: Regular or glare proof	To protect stitchery under glass	Hardware
HAMMER: Small tack hammer is best	To nail brads into frame when repairing it	Hardware
IRON AND IRONING BOARD	Padded board to steam press stitchery	Houseware

LINSEED OIL: Boiled and inedible	To finish frame in natural wood	Paint
MINERAL SPIRITS: See Turpentine	Can be used for the same purposes as turpentine (less expensive)	Paint or gas station
NAILS: Assorted sizes	To make wormwood holes in a frame	Hardware
PAINT AND VARNISH REMOVER	To remove any paint finishes	Paint
PAINTS: *Aluminum*	Seals in finish, prevents underneath color from bleeding through	Paint
Color in Oil comes in all colors in tubes *or*	For tinting paints For making glazes (antique)	Art supply
Universal Colorant, which comes in all colors in tubes	For tinting wood	Paint
Undercoat *or* flat, latex, casein type in white (can be tinted) and comes in colors	Can be used as first coat of paint for antiquing and other type finishes and textures	
Semi-gloss (eggshell finish or latex) in white and can be tinted, or comes in colors	For painting frames Can be used as first coat of paint for antiquing and other type finishes and textures	
Shellac or wood sealer	Seals in finish, prevents underneath color from bleeding through To seal or prime raw wood before applying finish	Paint
Spray comes in all colors and finishes, including varnish	To paint frames and dowel rods	Paint

Leaf Gold Liquid	To use on frames as a finish	Art supply
Metal Enamels comes in many colors including shades of gold, silver, copper and brass	To use as a finish on a frame For texture painting	Paint
Glazing Compound: to be mixed with flat undercoat paint and color	For antiquing	Paint

PAINTS:

Bronze Powders come in 200 colors, including many shades of gold, silver, which is aluminum, and copper	For adding high lights to antique finish For making glazes (antique) For adding highlights to a painted finish For making metal (bronze) base paints	Paint
Sulphur Powder or Burnt Umber mix Varnish, satin-type, clear or "rubbed effect" (dull finish)	To dull silver and other metallic finishes For a rubbed-effect finish To seal in paint color To protect a paint finish To use in making glazes (antique)	Drug or paint

PAPER:

Cardboard	Use 3 to 5 pieces (glued together) as a mat substitute	Boxes or laundry packings
Chipboard (gray cardboard) *or* corrugated paper	Backing for frame	Art, or laundry packings or boxes
Cleansing tissue	To sponge up droplets of adhesive and glue	Drug

Kraft brown wrapping paper *or* grocery bags (can be pressed)	To cover back of frame for final and professional look	Stationery
Matboard (heavy cardboard) single thickness recommended; comes in 16- by 20-inch pieces and larger sizes; also comes in many colors	Mat for mounting stitchery Mat to be covered	Art
Newspapers *or* plastic drop cloth	To protect surface where you are painting and working	Paint
PENCILS: No. 2 recommended Grease or Eyebrow	To draw lines on mats, paper, etc., before cutting To draw lines on glass and glazed surfaces	Stationery
PICTURE HANGERS: Bulldog	To place on back of frame for hanging in place of screw eyes and picture wire	Hardware
PICTURE HOOKS: Decorative (optional)	Place at top of frame as a decoration	Picture
PLASTER OF PARIS: Powder	For molding shape to be replaced on damaged frame	Drug or paint
POINTS: Diamond-shape staples (optional) POINT SETTER: Optional	To hold stitchery in frame in place of brads	Frame shop; glass
PRESS CLOTH: See-Thru-Steam-Thru (transparent and penetrating) *or* see-thru curtain fabric *or* piece of old sheet (both can be fireproofed)	To protect stitchery and fabric from scorching while steam pressing	Notions Drapery or yard goods

PUTTY: Plastic wood dough or wood putty powder	To mend frame To fill in nail holes	Paint
RAGS: Clean (old sheet)	To wash and wipe glass For antiquing Applying linseed oil to frame To keep in hands while mounting stitchery to keep it clean To keep fabric clean while gluing it to matboard	
RULER: Metal edge *or* T-square	To measure and cut fabric, cardboard, matboard, paper and etc.	Hardware
SANDER: Liquid	To soften paint finish before applying a new finish (fresh paint)	Paint
SCOTCHGARD: or other type protective fabric spray	To spray stitchery after steam pressing for protection of color and against soil before framing To protect covered mat against soil Framed stitchery can be sprayed at least once a year for protection if it does not have a glass on it	Notions
SCREW EYES: Metal loops at the end of a screw. Come ½ inch and longer. Size depends on thickness of frame	2 screw eyes needed on back of frame to attach wire for hanging	Hardware

SCREWS: Large size (wood)	To make deep scratches and grooves in frame for texture	Hardware
SHOE POLISH	To tint wood frames To paint wood frames	Shoe
SOAP: Mild liquid Bar *or* paraffin	For soaking and washing a stitchery For washing old frames For cleanup purposes To rub nails and brads; goes into wood easier	Grocery
SPONGES: Cellulose type or Natural	Use in back of sandpaper on a curved surface for sanding (makes it easier) For cleanup purposes To dampen press cloth while steam pressing	Grocery
SPOONS: Old teaspoons and tablespoons	For measuring purposes, including soap, vinegar, turpentine, varnish, etc.	
STEEL WOOL: Fine or Medium Coarse	To dull a paint finish To remove the shine from paint To smooth a finish For texture; to make scratch marks in wood	Paint
STICKS: Wood *or* cocktail stirrers *or* Dowel rods	Mixing paints and glazes	
STOVE BURNER OR HOT PLATE	To keep can of linseed oil hot while using it	
TAPE: Masking, ¾ inch or wider	To hold mounted stitchery in mat for frame	Paint

	To hold brads and support them in frame or diamond points	
	Can also serve as a finish in framing a stitchery if stitchery is mounted only and fits frame	
TOWELS: Terry cloth	To roll and absorb moisture after washing stitchery To cover stitchery design (raised) while steam pressing to keep from getting flat	Linens
TURPENTINE: Pure gum *or* mineral spirits	To mix glazes To thin oil base paints To thin color in oils and universal colorants For cleanup purposes after using oil base paints (hands and brushes)	
VASELINE OR SHORTENING	To grease shape before making mold of clay (for easy removal)	Drug or grocery
WIRE: Picture, which is braided steel and comes in different thicknesses to hold different weights	To pull through screw eyes on back of frame to hang stitchery	Hardware
WOOD: Dowel rods, come in different thicknesses; driftwood; tree branches; window-shade slats	To hang a stitchery	Lumber

BOOKS RECOMMENDED

ALEXANDER, MARY, *Handbook of Decorative Design and Ornament.* New York: Tudor Publishing Co., 1965.

ANDERS, NEDDA (CASSON), *Appliqué, old and new:* including patchwork and embroidery. New York: Hearthside Press, 1967.

BAGER, DR. BERTEL, *Nature as Designer.* New York: Van Nostrand Reinhold, 1966.

BEANEY, JAN, *The Young Embroiderer;* a how-it-is-done book of embroidery. New York: Frederick Warne & Co., Inc., 1966.

———, *Adventures with Collage.* New York: Frederick Warne & Co., Inc., 1970.

BEITLER, ETHEL JANE, *Create with Yarn: Hooking, Stitchery.* Scranton, Pa.: International Textbook Co., 1964.

BOLD, HAROLD C., *Plant Kingdom,* 3rd ed. Englewood Cliffs, N.J.: Prentice Hall, 1970.

BOSSERT, HELMUTH, *Folk Art of Primitive Peoples.* New York: Praeger, 1955.

BRIGHTMAN, FRANK H., and NICHOLSON, B. E., *Oxford Book of Flowerless Plants.* New York: Oxford University Press, 1966.

BUCHER, JO, *The Complete Guide to Embroidery Stitches and Crewel.* Des Moines, Ia.: Meredith Corp., 1971

BUTLER, ANNE, *Embroidery Stitches;* illustrated guide. New York: Praeger, 1968.

CARTER, J., *Creative Play with Fabrics and Threads.* Taplinger, 1969.

DE WIT, H. C. D., *Plants of the World (The Higher Plants II).* New York: E. P. Dutton & Co., Inc., 1966.

DILLMONT, THERESE DE, *Encyclopedia of Needlework,* New York: Joan Toggitt, Ltd.

DOWNER, MARION, *Discovering Design.* New York: Lothrop, Lee, and Shepard, 1947.

ENTHOVEN, JACQUELINE, *The Stitches of Creative Embroidery.* New York: Van Nostrand Reinhold, 1964.

———, *Stitchery for Children;* A Manual for Teachers, Parents and Children. New York: Van Nostrand Reinhold, 1968.

GUILD, VERA P., *Creative Use of Stitches.* Worcester, Mass.: Davis Publishers, Inc., 1969.

HARLOW, WILLIAM M., *Patterns of Life.* New York: Harper & Row, 1966.

Haupt, Battaglia Heidi, *Let's Embroider.* New York: Coward-McCann, 1938.

——, *Practical Embroidery.* Newton Centre, Mass.: Branford, 1963

Karasz, Mariska, *Adventures in Stitches.* New York: Funk & Wagnalls, 1959.

Krevitsky, Nik, *Stitchery: Art and Craft.* New York: Van Nostrand Reinhold, 1966.

Laury, Jean Ray, *Appliqué Stitchery.* New York: Van Nostrand Reinhold, 1966.

Meilach, Dona, and Snow, L. E., *Creative Stitchery.* Chicago: Reilly & Lee, Henry Regnery Co., 1970.

Miller, Irene Preston, and Lubell, Winifred, *The Stitchery Book.* New York: Doubleday & Company, Inc., 1965.

Nicholson, Joan, *Creative Embroidery.* New York: Gramercy Publishers, Inc., 1960.

Peterson, Grete, and Svennas, Elsie, *Handbook of Stitches;* 200 embroidery stitches, old and new, with descriptions, diagrams, and samplers. New York: Van Nostrand Reinhold, 1970.

Risley, Christine, *Creative Embroidery.* New York: Watson-Guptill, 1969.

Russell, P., *Lettering for Embroidery.* New York: Van Nostrand Reinhold, 1970.

Snook, Barbara, *Learning to Embroider.* New York: Hearthside Press, 1960.

——, *Needlework Stitches.* New York: Crown Publishers, Inc., 1963.

Springer, Jo, and Hedin, Solweig, *Creative Needlework.* New York: Arco, 1969.

Thomas, Mrs. Mary (Hedger), *Mary Thomas's Dictionary of Embroidery Stitches.* New York: Toggett, 1936.

Wilcox, Donald J., *New Design in Stitchery.* New York: Van Nostrand Reinhold, 1970.

Wilson, Erica, *Crewel Embroidery.* New York: Scribner's, 1962.

——, *Fun with Crewel Embroidery.* New York: Scribner's, 1965.

INDEX